FAITH AND FREEDOM BASIC READERS

This Is Our Valley
REVISED EDITION

Sister M. Marguerite, S.N.D., M.A.

Sister M. Bernarda, C.PP.S., PH.D.

GINN AND COMPANY
Boston • New York • Chicago • Atlanta
Dallas • Palo Alto • Toronto

© Copyright, 1963, by Ginn and Company
Copyright, 1953, 194, by Ginn and Company
Philippines Copyright, 1963, 1953, 1951, by Ginn and Company
All Rights Reserved

ACKNOWLEDGMENTS

Grateful acknowledgment is made to the following authors and publishers for permission to use copyrighted materials :
The Clarendon Press, Oxford, for an adaptation of "Crow Duv's Sunday," from *Legends of the Saints* by E. Lucia Turnbull.
Doubleday & Company, Inc., for "The Princess Who Could Not Cry," from *The Rainbow Cat* by Rose Fyleman, copyright 1923 by George H. Doran Company, reprinted by permission of Doubleday and Company, Inc., and The Society of Authors, literary representative of the Estate of the late Miss Rose Fyleman.
Ginn and Company for "Blessed Be God" by Sister Rose Margaret, C.S.J., from *We Sing and Dance* by Sister Cecilia, S.C. and others, copyright, 1957.
Harper & Row, Publishers for reprinting "Old Log House," from *A World to Know* by James S. Tippett, copyright 1933 by Harper & Brothers; also for "Familiar Friends," from *I Spend the Summer by* James S. Tippett, copyright 1930, Harper & Brothers and copyright 1958, James S. Tippett.
Alfred A. Knopf, Inc., for "Good Old Kristie," adapted from *Here Comes Kristie* by Emma L. Brock, by permission of Alfred A. Knopf, Inc., copyright, 1942 by Alfred A. Knopf, Inc.
The Macmillan Company for "If I Were a Tree," reprinted with the permission of the publisher from *Poems* by Rachel Field, copyright, 1924, 1930, 1957 by The Macmillan Company.
Sheed and Ward, Inc., for "Franz the Server," from *Terrible Farmer Timson and Other Stories by* Caryll Houselander, copyright 1957, Sheed & Ward, Inc.
The Estate of Rt. Rev. Hugh F. Blunt for "The King's Highway," from *A Lovely Gate Set Wide by* Sister Margaret Patrice, S.S.J.
Children's Playmate Magazine, Inc., and the authors for the following selections: L. F. Addington for "Tim Turner and the Fisherman," adapted from "Big Cherry Creek," July, 1952; Verna Turpin Borsky for "The Painted Cart," June, 1951; Miriam E. Mason for "The Strange Going-Away Present," adapted from "The Going-Away Kettle," October, 1951; Marjorie Pearson for "Pepper the Pony," adapted from the original story "The Cow Pony," April, 1951.
Highlights for Children, Inc., for permission to reprint and adapt the following selections: "The Thank-You Animals" by Anabel Armour, May, 1944; "Town and Country" by Marguerite Gode, September, 1945; "Saved at the Spring" by Florence L. Harwell, from "The Legend of Piasa Spring," September, 1944; "The Duck with Red Feet" by Sara Vance Miller, November, 1946; "The Princesses and Happy Village" by Kay Smith, September, 1947; all from *Children's Activities,* by permission of Highlights for Children, Inc., Columbus, Ohio, owner of the copyright.
Jack and Jill and the following authors for selections adapted and reprinted by special permission of and copyright by The Curtis Publishing Company: Marguerite Gallien for "Joseph and His Banty," from "Saved from the Storm," ©1958; Dorothy Patterson Gault for "Wanted: Two Kids," © 1959; Betsy Warren for "Beto's Many Sombreros," from "Beto and His Many Sombreros," © 1959; Ella Tunnell for "Off to the First Valley School," from "Wolf, Wolf," © 1957.
Story Parade, Inc., for "The Bicycle Tree" by Mildred Lawrence, copyright, 1947, by Story Parade, Inc., reprinted and adapted by permission; also for "Presents for Mother" by Robin Palmer, copyright,

1947, by Story Parade, Inc., re-printed and adapted by permission.

FAITH AND FREEDOM

NIHIL OBSTAT:
   Rev. Gerard Sloyan, S.T.L., PH.D., CENSOR DEPUTATUS

IMPRIMATUR:
   † Patrick A. O'Boyle, D.D., ARCHBISHOP OF WASHINGTON
   Washington, July 1, 1963

COMMISSION ON AMERICAN CITIZENSHIP
THE CATHOLIC UNIVERSITY OF AMERICA

Rt. Rev. Msgr. William J. McDonald, *President of the Commission*

Rt. Rev. Msgr. Joseph A. Gorham, *Director*

Katherine Rankin, *Editorial Consultant*

Sister Mary Lenore, O.P, *Curriculum Consultant*

PUBLISHED FOR THE CATHOLIC UNIVERSITY OF AMERICA PRESS
WASHINGTON, D.C.

Contents

■ Valley Folks

It May Be Hard to Believe		8
Town and Country, *a poem*	*Marguerite Gode*	16
The Treasure Hunt		17
The Duck with Red Feet	*Sara Vance Miller*	26
Tim Turner and the Fisherman	*L. F. Addington*	36
Strangers on the Road		44

■ Early Days in the Valley

The Magic Spring		54
Saved at the Spring	*Florence L. Harwell*	66
A Brave Little Indian Girl		72
The Strange Going-Away Present	*Miriam E. Mason*	78
Off to the First Valley School	*Ella Tunnell*	89
Old Log House, *a poem*	*James S. Tippett*	96

■ Prayer and Praise

Cousin Lorenzo Carries the News		98
Blessing the Seeds		108
Friend of the Farmer		114
Franz the Server	*Caryll Houselander*	122
Blessed Be God, a poem	*Sister Rose Margaret, C.S.J.*	138

■ Here Comes the Bookmobile

The Queen Bee	*Retold from Grimm*	140
The Wonderful Fortunes of a Woodcutter	*Hungarian Folk Tale*	149
The Princesses and Happy Village	*Kay Smith*	156
Nail Soup	*Swedish Folk Tale*	167
The Princess Who Could Not Cry	*Rose Fyleman*	174
Crom Duv's Sunday	*Retold by E. Lucia Turnbull*	183

■ Friendly Farmer Folks

The 4-H Club		194
The Bicycle Tree	*Mildred Lawrence*	200
If I Were a Tree, *a poem*	*Rachel Field*	212
The Chickens That Stayed Up		213
Presents for Mother	*Robin Palmer*	220
The Bread of Life		233

■ Valley Pets

Familiar Friends, *a poem*	*James S. Tippett*	242
Good Old Kristie	*Emma Brock*	244
Joseph and His Banty	*Marguerite Gallien*	252
Wanted : Two Kids	*Dorothy Patterson Gault*	261
Pepper the Pony	*Marjorie Pearson*	269

■ Friends from a Valley Far Away

Beto's Many Sombreros	*Betsy Warren*	278
The Painted Cart	*Verna Turpin Borsky*	287
The Thank-You Animals	*Anabel Armour*	296
Our Lady and the Indian		305
The King's Highway, *a poem*		
	Rt. Rev. Hugh F. Blunt, LL.D.	315

Illustrations by Bette Darwin, Sylvia Haggander, Tom Hill, Jack Jewell, Albert Jousset, William Plummer, Art Seiden.

Valley Folks

Far away from the city is a beautiful, quiet valley where many farmer folks—old and young—live and work together.

It May Be Hard to Believe

Good News

It was a beautiful, bright April morning in the valley. Mary Ann Brooks and her brother Andrew were waiting at Four Corners for the school bus. Suddenly they heard someone call.

"It's Billy," said Andrew as he turned around. "He seems very excited about something."

"Have you heard the news?" Billy shouted. "Larry and Patty Long have moved back to the valley."

"Oh, you're joking," said Mary Ann.

"No, I'm not," replied Billy. "It's really true. My father talked with Mr. Long yesterday. The Longs will be at school today."

"Why did they come back so soon? They just moved to the city a little over a year ago," said Mary Ann. "They even sold their home and farm and everything they had here."

"I wonder where they will live," said Andrew.

"Over by the old Mill Pond," replied Billy. "Mr. Long found a good piece of land there. He plans to have a dairy farm."

Just then a large yellow bus came along. The three excited children were still talking as they climbed in.

"What's up?" asked Charlie Burns, the bus man. "Is it someone's birthday? Why are you so excited?"

Billy, Andrew, and Mary Ann told the news to Charlie Burns and the children in the bus.

"I wonder what made the Long family change their minds about city life," said one of the older boys.

"Do you suppose that Larry and Patty really wanted to come back to the valley?" asked one of the girls. "In the city they went to a large Catholic school. Their father had a good job."

"Maybe Larry and Patty felt like the country mouse did when she went to the city," said Charlie Burns.

"Oh, I know that story," laughed Billy, and he began to tell the story.

The City Mouse and the Country Mouse

There was once a country mouse who had a friend who lived in the city.

One day the country mouse invited her friend to visit her. The country mouse took out everything she had to eat because she wanted to please her city friend. There was corn, wheat, and many kinds of seeds.

Now, the city mouse only turned up her nose at the food. She was used to having better food than seeds. She lived in a fine city house where she could get all kinds of cake, pie, cookies, and nuts.

"How is it, my friend," asked the city mouse, "that you can put up with such poor food as this? You are very foolish to live out here on this farm."

Then the city mouse said, "Why don't you come to the city? I will show you how you should live. You will never want to come back to the country."

The country mouse thought she might try city life for a while, and so the two mice started off to the city.

Late that evening they reached the fine house where the city mouse lived.

"You will want something to eat after your long trip," said the city mouse. She took her friend into the kitchen. There they found food left from a fine dinner.

Soon the country mouse was eating cakes, cookies, and other good things. She had just started thinking how much nicer this kind of life was when she saw two green eyes coming toward her.

"Run for your life!" cried the city mouse. "Here comes the cat."

Quick as a wink, the mice scampered through a hole in the floor.

"We were almost caught that time," said the city mouse, "but we are safe now."

"This is not the life for me," cried the country mouse at last.

The city mouse laughed and said, "If you live here, you must keep your eyes and ears open all the time."

"I'm much happier in my old barn," said the country mouse. "You may have better food than I do, but fine food does not make a happy home. It's better to eat seeds and live a long time in the country than to have fine food and live only a short time in the city."

Then the country mouse hurried back through the fields to her old barn.

The children laughed and clapped their hands when Billy finished his story.

The bus stopped, and the children were still talking excitedly as they started toward Holy Cross School. There in the schoolyard were Patty and Larry Long waiting for them.

"Hello, everybody," Larry and Patty called, and at once all the children started talking to them.

"Are the city mice glad to be back in the country?" asked Andrew.

"Oh, yes, we are," Patty answered. "Everything out here is so beautiful and different from the hot old city."

"Didn't you like living in the city?" asked Mary Ann.

"Oh, it was fun when we first moved there," Patty said. "We liked the tall buildings, the busy airport, the parks, and the playgrounds. After a while, we missed the birds and flowers."

"We even missed the cows, pigs, and chickens," said Larry, "but we missed our valley friends most of all."

"Well, some city mice really do like the country," said Billy.

"And we're all glad you've come back to the valley," said Andrew.

Town and Country

The town has a store
And a church with a steeple,
Streets full of houses
And hurrying people.
It's noisy with whistles
And bells that ring,
And yellow canaries
That loudly sing.

The country is quiet
And patchworked with trees,
And paths that go winding
Wherever they please.
It's covered with daisies
And cool with shade,
And blue with puddles
Where feet can wade.

Marguerite Gode

The Treasure Hunt
On Pirate's Shore

Pirate's Shore was on the sandy bank of a wide creek.

Patty and Larry Long were there on Saturday morning early—long before the others came for the treasure hunt.

Patty watched the birds as they flew between the trees. She saw squirrels and chipmunks scamper out of the woods. Once in a while she and Larry saw a frog jump into the water. Young rabbits hopped through the bushes without even stopping to look at the children.

"Oh, I am so happy to be in the country," said Patty.

"We could never have a treasure hunt like this in the city," said Larry.

Just then they heard fierce cries. "Yo-ho-ho!" said make-believe pirates as they ran toward Patty and Larry.

"Yo-ho-ho, pirates," answered Larry and Patty, returning the pirate salute. "Are you ready to hunt for treasure?"

Each pirate had a band of red cloth around his head. Even Scout, Billy's dog, had a red cloth around his neck. Some of the pirates carried flags. Billy and Andrew had spades with them.

"We can dig up all kinds of treasure with these spades," said Billy.

"We must work fast to find all the treasure in the valley," said Andrew.

Patty smiled in her happy way. "I wish we could find a *real* treasure," she said. "Just think of what we could do with a pot of gold!"

The boys and girls started talking about the different things they would do if they found a real treasure.

Carl Singer would build a bigger and better house and barn. He and his sister Theresa lived in a small white house near Pirate's Shore.

Others decided they would buy new machines to help do the farm work.

Theresa laughed as she said, "I guess you'll think this is strange, but I would buy a new coat—one that was really mine, not one that my older sister could no longer wear."

As the pirates ran down a path they sang their club song.

"Pirates are we,
So fierce and strong;
Pirates are we,
Oh, hear our song.
We dig in the ground for hidden gold.
Soon we'll carry home
All our arms can hold.
Look out! Take care!
Pirates are we!
Yo-ho-ho! Yo-ho-ho! Yo-ho-ho!"

The children looked for a long time, but they did not find any treasure. They did find a good spot to sit down and rest and eat their picnic lunches.

After they had eaten their lunches, Larry put his head back and looked up toward the sky.

"Look at the strange-looking hole in that tree," he said. "What kind of animal do you suppose lives in it?"

"It's a bee tree!" cried Billy.

"Do you suppose there is any honey in it?" asked Theresa.

"Why don't we stick a spade into the hole and find out?" asked Mary Ann.

"That's a dangerous idea," replied Billy. "That hole may be alive with hundreds of bees. My grandfather found a bee tree on the other side of the creek last year. It was filled with honey, but it was also filled with bees."

"Let's run back and tell your father about it," Andrew said to Billy. "He used to keep bees. He can tell us how to get the honey out of the tree."

Bees and Honey

The pirates lost no time in running to Billy's farm. Mr. Butterfield was busy, but he stopped and listened to the excited children. Soon they were on their way back to the tree.

When he saw the tree, Mr. Butterfield said, "This tree is rich in honey. The swarm has been here for a long time."

"How can you tell that, Dad?" Billy asked.

"I can tell by the signs," answered his father. "See how smooth the bark is around the hole. That shows that it has been used a long time."

Then Billy's father winked at the children and said, "Well, it looks as if you have found an exciting treasure. Beekeepers sometimes look for days and days before they find such a fine swarm of bees."

"Can we get the honey out of the tree now?" Larry wanted to know.

Mr. Butterfield thought for a moment. Then he answered, "First, we will have to make another home for the bees. It will have to be a good-sized hive. It is really more important to catch a swarm of bees than to get the honey, but I think we can do both."

Mr. Butterfield had some old beehives at his house. With the pirates' help, it didn't take long to get one of the hives ready.

Mr. Butterfield, his two older sons, and the pirates went back again to the creek. They cut out the part of the tree with the bees in it and took it to the new hive.

They blew smoke into the old nest to make the bees come out. The bees fell near an opening in the hive. Slowly they started going into the beehive. Soon the new beehive was swarming with bees.

"This hive belongs to all of you,"

Mr. Butterfield told the pirates. "I will show you how to take care of the bees. Whatever honey you get from them is yours to eat or to sell."

24

"Let's take turns caring for the beehive," said Carl. "If we are all going to share the honey, we should all share the work too."

"We'll use the money we get from selling the honey for our club," said Andrew. "Maybe someday we'll have enough to buy some of the things we need for camping."

"Hurrah!" shouted all the pirates.

"Bow-wow," barked Scout.

Then they took the honey from the bee tree. There was plenty of golden honey for all of the pirates. They thanked Billy's father for helping them. Later the pirates had a feast of fresh milk, homemade bread, and honey.

They had really found a treasure at Pirate's Shore.

The Duck with Red Feet
Quacky's Big Idea

Mr. Quackenbush and his wife lived on a small farm in Honey Spring Valley. Quacky, as his wife and friends called him, took care of his farm animals and cherry trees and worked in his garden.

Mrs. Quackenbush kept the small house clean, and she cooked wonderful meals. When she had time, she sewed and made her own clothes.

Their life had been quiet and happy until the day Quacky decided to try to make Honey Spring Valley a famous place. He got the idea from watching special TV shows.

Of course, Quacky told his wife what he had decided to do. She thought his idea was very silly, and she didn't get at all excited about it.

One Friday morning Quacky found a strange-looking bug in his garden. He was sure there wasn't another one like it in the country. He decided to send it to the county inspector. While Quacky was looking for a box, the bug flew away.

That afternoon Quacky's mule jumped over the fence. "Now, that's what I call a high jump," cried Quacky. "I'm sure no other mule in the world can jump that high. Here's something to make Honey Spring Valley famous."

He decided to take the mule to the county animal show, but the mule never jumped again. So Quacky had to give up that idea.

Quacky was digging potatoes on the following Monday morning when he found a very large one.

"My, that's almost as large as a pumpkin," he said to himself. "I think I'll send it to the county fair. It will surely make Honey Spring Valley a very famous place."

While Quacky was carrying the potato to the house he dropped it, and it rolled down into the well.

One day something really did happen to make Quacky feel happy and excited about his idea. He was busy picking cherries when suddenly he stopped. An unusual duck was coming toward him.

"Am I seeing things?" he wondered. "That duck's legs are yellow, but he has two red feet. I wonder why I never saw that before. At last, I have found something that will make the valley famous!"

Quacky wanted to hurry into the house and tell the good news to his wife, but he had tried that before. She had always laughed at him.

"It may be better to keep quiet about this unusual duck," he told himself. "I'll let my wife be surprised when she reads about it in the newspaper."

With the unusual duck under his arm, Quacky hurried over to see his friend Hans Hopper. Hans was busy working in his garden when Quacky came along with the duck.

"Why, this is the strangest duck I've ever seen," said Hans. "You should tell the county inspectors about him."

That very evening Quacky sat down and wrote a long letter to the county inspectors.

After a few days he received an answer telling him to send the duck with the red feet to the inspectors. Now, Quacky was so proud and so happy that he could hardly talk. He couldn't wait until his neighbors in the valley and the whole county heard about his duck.

Trouble Starts

One Wednesday evening something happened. When Quacky went into the house at suppertime, his wife asked, "What's all this talk about the county inspectors and a duck with red feet?"

"Why, who has been talking to you?" asked Quacky in a surprised voice.

"Hans Hopper's wife," answered Mrs. Quackenbush. "She called and said that the county inspectors stopped to pick up Hans. They are on their way over here, and they are as angry as wet roosters."

"Why should they be angry?" asked. Quacky.

"I'm not sure," his wife replied. "Hans' wife just said that you had played a joke on the inspectors."

For a few moments Quacky did not say a word. Finally he told his wife about the unusual duck.

"Oh, Quacky, how foolish! That is not an unusual duck," said his wife. "Last week our neighbor was painting his dairy barn, and that duck went into his yard and stepped into red paint."

Before Quacky could say another word, a car pulled up to the house.

"Oh! What shall I do?" cried Quacky.

"You just keep the men talking and let me take care of everything else," said his wife as she left the room.

When Hans Hopper and the county inspectors walked into the house, one of them said to Quacky, "You think you're being funny, don't you? You painted that duck's feet red and then tried to make us believe that you owned an unusual kind of bird. We'll fix you for this."

The inspectors were so angry that Quacky had little trouble making them talk. On and on they went.

Soon wonderful smells came from the kitchen, and one of the inspectors said, "Say, I smell something good."

"That's baked ham," said Quacky. "My wife bakes the most delicious ham in the world."

"Don't I smell homemade bread?" asked the other inspector.

Just then the door opened. There stood Mrs. Quackenbush in a lovely pink apron and with a big smile on her face.

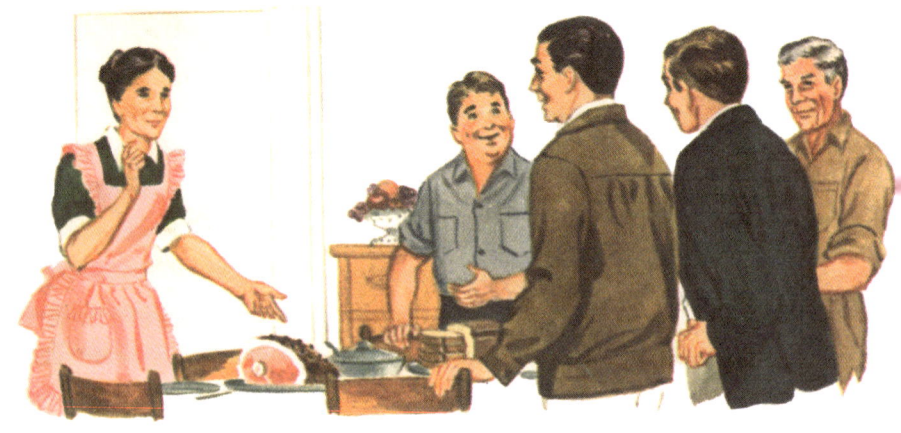

"Won't you folks have supper with us?" she asked in her friendly way. "You must be hungry by this time."

"Why, yes," replied both inspectors together. "We would like that."

"I've never tasted such good bread as this," said Hans Hopper, as they started eating the delicious meal.

"The ham is the best I have ever eaten," said one of the inspectors.

Before long the inspectors were very friendly. "You know," said one of them to Quacky's wife, "Mr. Quackenbush was telling us about the mistake he made with his duck. It's really a good joke, isn't it?"

When the meal was finished, the happy county inspectors thanked Mrs. Quackenbush.

Then one of them said, "I think you are the best cook in the whole world. Would you be willing to be on our TV program next month? The program will tell people about all the many ways to enjoy farm life."

"You could also help to write our new farm cookbook," said the other inspector.

"I'll be glad to do whatever I can," answered Mrs. Quackenbush.

The two inspectors left the house and rode off.

"Well, it wasn't my duck or my bug or my potato that made Honey Spring Valley famous," said Quacky to his wife. "It was your cooking. Now, who would ever have thought that things would turn out like this!"

Sara Vance Miller

Tim Turner and the Fisherman

One Saturday Tim Turner stood by the mailbox and watched the mail truck go down the road. He felt unhappy and disappointed because the mailman had not left him a letter or even a card. It could have been an important letter, too.

Tim sighed as he walked back toward the house where he lived with his mother and a younger sister. He stopped when his quick ears caught the sound of a car. It was a large blue station wagon, coming up the road toward Tim's house.

The car stopped in front of the mailbox, and a man looked at the name on the mailbox.

"John Turner," the man whispered.

"That's my father's name," said Tim. "He's dead now, but Mother won't take the name off the box. It's just another way to remember my dad."

Are you, perhaps, Tim Turner?" the man asked.

"Yes, sir," Tim replied eagerly. He thought maybe the man knew something about his letter. A moment later his hopes fell, and he knew he was wrong.

"I want to go fishing in the creek near Rock Hills," said the man. "They told me down the road that Tim Turner could show me the way. How about it?"

Tim didn't answer. He could hear the cow over in the pasture. It was his job to clean the barn and milk the cow on Saturdays.

"They say that it's a long way to the hills," said the man, "and that the road is rough."

"That's right, sir," replied Tim, "but the fishing is always good in that part of the creek."

"Do you enjoy fishing?" the man asked.

"Yes," answered Tim, "but right now I need a job more than I need to go fishing."

"What kind of job?" the man asked.

"I read in the paper that they want a boy to sell the *Farm News* magazine in Honey Spring Valley," Tim said. "I wrote and asked for the job. They wrote back and asked me to give the names of people who know me and could tell what kind of boy I am. I haven't heard one word since. Maybe I didn't give the right names. Yet I named my aunt and uncle and my pastor. They all know me."

"Perhaps I should tell you my name," said the man. "I am Hubert Judge."

Tim shook hands and said, "I'm pleased to know you, Mr. Judge."

"Now can we get started on our way to the creek?" Mr. Judge asked.

"As soon as I milk the cow and ask my mother," answered Tim.

"Can't someone else milk the cow?" Mr. Judge asked.

"Yes, my mother could," replied Tim, "but I don't think I should ask her. She sews and bakes for other people all week, just to make a living for us."

"Well, all right," said Mr. Judge. "I'll wait around here while you milk the cow, but hurry, won't you?"

39

Mr. Judge talked to Mrs. Turner while Tim finished his chores. His mother said that he could show Mr. Judge the way to Rock Hills. So Tim got his fishing pole, a net, and a can of worms from the barn. Then he and Mr. Judge started off toward Rock Hills.

"Now, tell me, son," said Mr. Judge, "why are you so eager to get that job selling magazines?"

"To earn some money and help my mother," answered Tim. "If I can earn enough, I can also buy a bicycle. Then I could get to more homes in the valley."

When they reached the hills, they saw a few large squirrels and some rabbits.

"I have a gun in my car," Mr. Judge told Tim. "If we don't catch any fish, maybe we can do a little hunting."

"Oh, no sir," replied Tim. "This is not the right time for hunting. It would be against the law to hunt now."

"Who would ever know about it?" asked the man, watching Tim carefully.

"The little squirrels and bunnies would, sir," answered Tim. "This is the time of the year when the mother squirrels and rabbits are caring for their babies in the nests. If the mothers are killed, the babies will not have food and will die. That's why it's against the law to hunt at this time of the year."

"Hmm," said the man.

When they finally got to the creek, Mr. Judge put on his high boots and walked out into the water with Tim.

Before long they had each caught a nice large fish.

Later in the day, Mr. Judge walked up the stream where the water was rougher. By this time, both he and Tim were tired. So they sat down on a big rock to rest.

"This gives me time to talk to you," said Mr. Judge. "I have something important to tell you."

Tim looked eager and surprised.

"I am the one who asked for a boy to sell the *Farm News* magazine," Mr. Judge said. "Three other boys have already asked for the job. I asked each one of them to come here and fish."

"You did? Why?" asked Tim.

"To find out what kind of boys they are," replied Mr. Judge. "I need a boy who is cheerful, willing to work, and obeys laws. Not one of the other boys would show me the way to Rock Hills. They said the road was too rough, and it was too far to walk. So, my boy, you have the job."

Tim could hardly speak. For a moment he kept still. Then finally he looked at Mr. Judge and said, "Thank you, sir. I can hardly wait to tell Mother."

With a big smile on his face Tim ran almost all the way to the Turner farm with Mr. Judge following him.

L. F. Addington

Strangers on the Road

The Lost Cow

Andrew Brooks' father came into the house one morning looking very worried.

"Our new cow has gone through the fence and run away," he said. "She may wander far off and get lost or hurt."

"I'll go out and look for her," said Andrew. He was glad to have a good reason for getting out in the warm sunshine. "I'll ask Carl Singer and Billy Butterfield to help me."

So Andrew went off whistling a cheerful tune. He went to Carl's house first. Carl was glad to help Andrew.

Billy was working in his vegetable garden when Carl and Andrew came by. Billy planned to send some of his carrots to the county fair. He, too, was glad to leave his work for a while and help Andrew find the runaway cow.

The three boys stopped at each farm to ask if anyone had seen Flossy the cow. Now and then they stopped to listen for the ting-a-ling of her bell.

When the boys went past the Hunts' house, Jack Hunt was standing beside the barn in the pasture.

He saw the boys go by, but he did not say anything to them. So they did not speak to him. His younger sister Jenny was in the front yard drying her hair, and she spoke to the boys.

"Have you seen a lost cow?" Andrew called to her. "She is red with short horns and has a bell around her neck. Her name is Flossy."

Jenny shook her wet head and called back, "I haven't seen any lost cows."

Jack heard what the boys said. "They didn't even ask me about the cow," he thought. "They never ask me to play with them or to join their pirate club."

Jack's father had once had a quarrel with some valley farmers. It had been so long ago that almost everyone had forgotten what the quarrel was about, but it was the reason why many valley people were not friendly with the Hunts.

"A quarrel is like a stone wall that keeps people apart," Mr. Hunt had often said.

More than anything else in the world, Jack wanted to make friends with some of the boys in the valley, but he was afraid to try. He really didn't even know how to begin. He felt lonely and unhappy as he watched the boys go on their way.

As the three boys walked on down the road they suddenly heard something.

"Somebody is having car trouble," cried Carl.

"Look, it's a car with a strange-looking trailer," said Billy.

For a few moments the boys forgot about the lost cow. They hurried toward the trailer. Two priests were standing beside it, trying to decide what to do.

"We're mighty glad to see you," said one of the priests when he saw the boys. "You're an answer to prayer. We're having car trouble. Is there a gas station anywhere around here?"

"Not out this way, Father," replied Carl.

"Well, is there a telephone somewhere around here?" asked the taller priest.

The three boys looked at each other, and Carl said, "Yes, there is a house just up the road. The people who live there are named Hunt."

"Would one of you be kind enough to run up to that house and ask someone to call a gas station for us?" asked the other priest.

The boys looked at each other again. No one wanted to go to the Hunts' house. Finally Andrew offered to go.

Finding Help

Jack was still by the barn when Andrew got to the Hunts' house. After Andrew told Jack about the trouble, he asked if he could use his phone.

"Perhaps Dad should go down and see if he can help first," said Jack.

As soon as Mr. Hunt heard about the priests having car trouble he got out his truck. He took some gas and some tools along with him.

"Jump in and ride along with me," he told the boys.

As they were riding along, Andrew told Jack that he was out looking for a lost cow when they met the priests.

Jack felt a little ashamed as he said, "I think I know where your cow is. I saw a strange cow in the pasture behind our chicken house. She'll be safe there until we get back. I will help you catch her."

"You will?" asked Andrew in a surprised voice. "Oh, that's nice of you."

Mr. Hunt found out what was wrong with the motor of the car. With his tools he had it fixed in only a short time.

Then the priests told who they were. "My name is Father Gardener," said the taller of the two priests, "and this is Father Francis. We are on our way to give a mission up in the hill country. This trailer is really a motor chapel."

"You mean it looks like a church inside?" Billy asked.

"That's right. It does," replied Father Gardener, showing them the altar.

"You see, there is no church up in the hill country. So we take our chapel there," Father Francis told the boys.

"Are there Catholics living there?" asked Andrew in surprise.

"That's right," replied Father Francis. "There are many Catholics, living in out-of-the-way places, who can't get to Mass on Sundays. Sometimes there is no priest to offer the Mass, or the church is miles and miles away. That's why we go there once or twice each year."

Father Gardener smiled, and he said, "We're called motor missionaries."

The boys wanted to know more about motor missionaries, but the priests had to leave.

When the boys got back to the Hunts' house, Jack helped them to catch Flossy. He even gave them a rope to use.

Carl, Andrew, and Billy were beginning to think that Jack really was a friendly boy. Just then Mrs. Hunt invited them to have some ice-cold milk and cookies.

The boys thanked Mrs. Hunt. While they were eating their cookies Billy said, "It's too bad that you live so far away, Jack. I think you might enjoy our treasure hunts."

"Say, couldn't you ride your bicycle down to the creek?" asked Carl.

"I guess I could," answered Jack slowly. "Could I really become a pirate?"

"Well, you found Flossy for us," said Andrew. "You just may find all kinds of treasures at Pirate's Shore. Our next treasure hunt will be on Saturday."

"I'll be there," said Jack, and he smiled for the first time that day.

Early Days in the Valley

The valley folks often told the children these stories about the early days in Honey Spring Valley.

The Magic Spring

The Orphans

Long ago the valley was a great forest. Many Indians lived under the tall trees.

Here and there lived a pioneer family of white people. They were not born there, but they had come to the valley to build homes and raise their food. The pioneers always tried to find a spring of good water. They usually put up their cabins close to the spring.

In one of these pioneer cabins lived a father with his three children who were named Catherine, Melissa, and Mark. Their mother had died soon after they moved to the valley, and so the children had a lot of hard work to do.

Near their cabin was a clear, sparkling spring. In the summer the water in the spring was ice cold, but in the winter it never froze.

For a while things went well for the family, but then hard times came. For weeks and weeks there was no rain. The corn died in the fields because of the hot sun. Wild rabbits came in from the woods at night and ate many of the small plants.

The pioneer father knew that his children would be hungry during the winter if he did not go to hunt food in the forest. When the cold weather came, he took his gun and started out.

"I shall be gone for weeks," he told his children. "I am going to meet some men on the other side of the valley. It is safer for us to hunt together. You will have enough food until I come back."

His brave children were not afraid, for they could take care of themselves. They could catch fish in the river. There was plenty of cornmeal in the barrels. There would be enough to eat until their father returned.

Soon a sad thing happened. The Indians were very angry because the white men were hunting in their forest. A terrible fight took place, and most of the pioneer men and many of their Indian enemies were killed.

Catherine, Melissa, and Mark waited and waited. Mark cut wood and kept the cabin warm. Catherine, who was the oldest, cooked a little cornmeal every day, but each time she looked into the barrel she felt frightened.

"There is hardly enough cornmeal to last through the winter," she thought.

The pioneer children were not the only ones who were having a hard time. Many Indians were orphans because their fathers had also been killed in the fight.

There were five poor Indian orphans who were wandering through the cold, dark woods, eating berries and whatever else they could find. At night they would sleep under the trees or in caves.

One night the snow fell and covered the ground, and the berries were gone. The five orphans wandered through the forest until they were almost frozen and very hungry.

When morning came, they could hardly walk. Finally they saw smoke coming from a log cabin. They knew that this was a white man's house, and they were afraid.

"The white men are not our friends," they whispered to one another. "They took our hunting grounds, and they killed our fathers."

"Perhaps they would let us come in and get warm," cried the smallest orphan. She was a tiny girl with big dark eyes.

After a while the children became brave enough to knock on the door.

An Answered Prayer

When Catherine opened the door, she saw the Indian children. "Go away," she shouted angrily as she started closing the door.

Melissa, her younger sister, had a kinder heart. "Please let them come in just to get warm," she begged.

Melissa kept on begging until Catherine let the children come into the house.

"How hungry they look!" said Mark. "They are as thin as little birds."

"We, too, are hungry," said Catherine in an unfriendly way.

"The tiny girl is so frightened," Melissa whispered to Catherine. "May we share a little of our cornmeal with her, just a little?"

"There is not even enough meal in the barrel to last us for a week!" Catherine cried.

"I don't want to eat if we don't give them something," said Mark as he began to put more wood on the fire. "It's too cold for them to go on. We have to do something for them."

Mark thought for a long time. "Remember, when our mother did not know what to do, she always prayed and asked God to help her to do the right thing," said Mark. "Perhaps, if we say a prayer, God will help us to decide."

The pioneer children knelt before a crucifix and prayed while the Indian children looked at them in wonder.

When they finished praying, Catherine spoke softly, "We will share what we have. Go, Mark, and bring some water from the spring. Melissa, get some dishes from the chest."

Catherine hung a large iron pot over the fire and started to cook the cornmeal.

Suddenly Melissa cried in a loud voice, "Look, Catherine, look!"

She had opened the large wooden chest where the family kept some dishes and other things. There were no dishes in it, but the chest was full of rich cornmeal. The children had not known it was there.

Another surprising thing happened at the spring. As Mark put his bucket into the cold water, he saw that a large tree had fallen during the night. A hole in the tree was full of honey. There were buckets and buckets of delicious honey in the tree.

Nobody ever tasted more delicious honey than that from the old tree. "It is like magic," the children often said. "No matter how much of it we eat, there is always some left. We will never get tired of it. It's like a magic spring of honey."

All that winter the pioneer and Indian orphans lived together in the log cabin. They soon became true friends.

They were no longer in danger of going hungry. The Indian boys helped to catch fish and wild rabbits for food. The Indian girls knew what kinds of fruit and berries were good to eat.

Catherine often told how God had answered their prayers when they called on Him.

"He must be a very kind Father," said one of the Indian children. "Could we call Him our Father, too?"

The pioneer children taught the Indians how to make the Sign of the Cross and to pray the Our Father. They told them about the Son of God and His love for little children, and every day the pioneer orphans and the Indian orphans knelt to say their prayers together.

As the years passed, more and more pioneer men and women came to make their homes in the valley. Log cabins, the tall trees, and the Indians slowly disappeared.

The story of the magic honey spring lived on and became known all over the valley. That is how the valley came to be known as Honey Spring Valley.

Saved at the Spring

One summer the valley was hot, dry, and dusty. There had been no rain for months. All the streams and creeks had dried up.

Wild animals had died by the hundreds that summer, and the poor Indians had nothing to eat. Many of them were sick.

One small Indian boy, Feather Foot, lived in the valley with his grandfather, who was called Brave Bear. Day after day the Indian child lay on the floor of their wigwam, weak and sick.

"Water, Grandfather! Please give me some water," Feather Foot begged over and over.

Brave Bear listened until he could stand it no longer. He decided to go into the forest to look for water. He, too, was weak because there was nothing to eat or drink.

Before he left, the old man threw his water bag over his shoulder, strapped it on, and started walking down the dry river bed.

Brave Bear remembered having seen a little spring of water somewhere near the hills, but he was sure that it, too, had dried up after the long, hot summer.

Oh, if only he could find some water somewhere!

After walking many miles, Brave Bear came to a clearing near the hills. He looked around, but he could not see a sign of water anywhere.

Gasping from weakness after his long day's walk, Brave Bear lay on the ground to rest. Suddenly he heard something in the bushes nearby.

Very quietly he got up and looked through the leaves. The moon and the stars were bright, and the old Indian could see a mother deer and two little fawns picking their way secretly down the hill.

The mother deer seemed to know there was danger nearby. Every once in a while she stopped, raised her head, and sniffed the air.

Brave Bear kept very still. He thought the deer must be taking her fawns to water. He planned to wait and see where she went. Then he would kill her with his strong arrow. He would not only have water for his grandchild, but he would also have food.

The old Indian watched and waited. The mother deer went toward the bottom of the hill. Suddenly she stopped, raised her head, and again sniffed the air.

After she pushed some of the bushes to one side, Brave Bear could see a spring of clear, sparkling water.

Bravely the mother deer stood beside each little fawn as it took a long drink.

Twice, she raised her head, looked around, and sniffed the air. Then she took a long, cool drink.

All during this time Brave Bear's hand was tightly on his bow. His arrow was ready to fly on its way.

Then he thought, "How tired and hungry that deer must be! Still she is caring for her little ones. What will happen to them if I kill their mother?"

The old Indian's hand fell to his side and with it, the bow and arrow. He would save the life of the mother deer who had shown him the way to the spring.

He watched the deer and two fawns turn and go back up into the hills. Brave Bear went over and knelt by the spring. He drank and drank. He filled the water bag to the very top.

Soon he began to feel stronger, and his body seemed to have new life in it.

In the moonlight the old Indian raised his hands to heaven and asked the Great Spirit to bless the spring that had saved his life and that of his grandchild.

Then the old man hurried back to the wigwam. How eagerly little Feather Foot drank the cool water! Soon he, too, felt stronger.

When the other Indians heard about the spring near the hills, they went to get water. Before they left, Brave Bear made them promise that they would never, never raise a bow to shoot a deer.

They could hunt bears, rabbits, wild geese, and squirrels, but the deer were to be saved.

Florence L. Harwell

A Brave Little Indian Girl

In the early days of Honey Spring Valley there were Indians living in many parts of our country. One was a little Indian girl named Tekakwitha, who lived in a village far away.

The child's mother was a kind Christian woman who believed in the true God and loved Him very much. Her father was a strong and brave man, but he did not believe in God, the Father of Jesus.

When the father went hunting or down the river on a fishing trip, the Indian mother would tell Tekakwitha and her younger brother about the good God.

Little Tekakwitha loved to hear stories about the God of the Christians, but over and over again her mother told her never to let her father know that she was learning about Jesus, the Son of God.

Although the brave Indian loved his wife and children, he would not let them speak about Christ, the Son of God. He would never allow them to see a priest when one came to the village. That is why Tekakwitha and her brother had never been baptized.

Once a terrible sickness came to the village, and many people died from it.

Early one morning, the little girl saw her mother crying. "The sickness has come to our home," said the squaw. "Little Brother is very, very ill."

That day Little Brother died. Then Tekakwitha and her parents were all taken sick. Soon sad times came for the little girl.

God took both her mother and father from her. She was left all alone in the world. The lonely little girl could not live by herself, so her uncle, who was a great Indian chief, took her to his home.

The chief loved Tekakwitha, but he would not let her speak about God, the Father of Jesus Christ.

Every day the child had to say her prayers in secret. Sometimes she ran off to the mission chapel to visit Our Lord in His forest home. No matter how hard she tried, Tekakwitha could not keep her secret from her two aunts. When they found out that she believed in Jesus Christ, they treated her cruelly.

All this time the Indian girl kept her love for the Son of God. She told all her troubles and sorrows to Him and His holy Mother. Still she was not yet a real Christian because she had never been baptized.

Each day Tekakwitha seemed to grow more and more unhappy, and her uncle became worried about her. When he found out the reason for her sorrow, he said she could be baptized.

At once Tekakwitha ran to the mission chapel and told the good news to the priest. Several months later she was baptized and was named Catherine.

Now life became harder than ever for the new Christian Indian.

Her aunts were cruel to her. They refused to allow her to go to Mass, and if she went, they gave her nothing to eat all day.

Catherine Tekakwitha did not mind being treated this way. She knew Christ had suffered and died for her, and she was glad to suffer for Him.

After some time the Indians who were not Christians burned down the mission chapel. They would no longer allow a priest to come to the village.

Many of those who believed in the true God could not stand this. They left the village and went to live with Christians far up the river. Tekakwitha also wanted to leave, but every time she asked her uncle to let her go, he refused.

One night, while he was away on a hunting trip, Tekakwitha and a friend got into a canoe.

They started off to find a new home with other Christians. Now, when Catherine Tekakwitha and her friend reached the village, they were free to love and serve the true God as they wished.

For three years Catherine spent a holy and happy life in the village. Then one day she became very ill. It was easy to see that she would soon die. Each day people came to visit her and to pray at her bedside.

On Tuesday of Holy Week the greatest of all Friends came to the Indian girl as she prepared for death. The next day she was with Our Lord in His heavenly home.

Several moments after her death Catherine Tekakwitha's face became so beautiful that those who saw it cried out in wonder. People now knew that another soul had gone to heaven or, as the Indians called it, "the happy hunting ground."

The Strange Going-Away Present
A Bargain

"We're going to move far away," said a pioneer father one day to his family. "We're going to a place called Honey Spring Valley. It's a new part of the country, and life may be very hard there."

Marie, his daughter, was so excited that her eyes danced.

"Perhaps, now that we're going to move to a new part of the country, I'll get a gun," she said. "Grandfather may give me one as a going-away present."

Marie had no sisters, but she had six brothers. Each of them, even the very youngest, had a gun of his own. Marie wanted a gun, too. She had asked for one for her birthday, but she had only received thread, a sewing basket, a rag doll, and a fluffy kitten.

When her grandfather and grandma brought her a going-away present, Marie was disappointed. It was only a little brass kettle with a handle on it.

"What can I do with this?" Marie asked every time she looked at it.

Her brothers, of course, thought it was a good joke. "It will make a nice little milk pail," they told her. "Bossy would be proud to have a brass kettle used at milking time."

This, too, was a joke because Bossy, the cow, was cross and mean. No one even wanted to milk her.

Marie enjoyed the trip to Honey Spring Valley. She loved riding in the covered wagon.

When the family finally reached the valley, Marie's father and her brothers started building a log cabin. Several of the pioneers, who already lived in the valley, helped them. They told Marie's father that the valley land was wonderful.

There was only one thing they did not like. Many wolves were in the forest.

"We won't mind the wolves," said Marie's father to his sons. "After all, we have seven men in this cabin, and each one has his own gun."

Now more than ever Marie wished for a gun. Every time she even spoke about it to her father, he would say, "Marie, remember that you are a girl. Stay in the house and help your mother with the housework and sewing. Your brothers and I will kill the wolves."

Jim's chore at their new home was to milk Bossy, but he did not like it. He would rather hunt for wild animals.

One day Jim made a bargain with his sister Marie. He knew how much she wanted a gun. "If you will milk Bossy for me, I will hunt for a wolf and give you the money that I get for it. Then, if Father doesn't mind, maybe you can buy a gun," Jim said.

The storekeeper had already told Jim that he would give him ten dollars for every wolf he killed.

"That's a bargain!" Marie cried with delight.

Every day Marie milked the cross old cow while Jim went hunting for wolves. Day after day went by, and nobody had even seen any wolves. So Jim, of course, did not shoot any.

Soon Marie found that she really did not mind milking Bossy. The cow even seemed to like Marie, for she was no longer cross and mean. She no longer shook her horns at Marie, and she even stopped knocking over the milk bucket.

"I'm going to miss milking you when Jim kills a wolf," Marie told Bossy one day.

On the Fourth of July there was to be a big shooting match in the valley. Marie's father and brothers planned to be in it.

"How I wish I could go to the shooting match with the boys!" sighed Marie.

"Little ladies don't do things like that," her mother told her.

On the Fourth of July the boys were up before daylight. They and their father left early for the shooting match.

"Take care of Bossy for me," Jim said to Marie as he put on his cap. "If I win a prize at the shooting match, I'll bring it back tonight, and you can have it."

Later that morning a neighbor came into the yard. His wife was ill, and he wanted Marie's mother to come over at once.

"You won't be afraid to stay here alone, will you, Marie?" her mother asked.

"Oh, no, Mother," Marie answered.

A Visitor

After her mother had left, Marie did a little sewing. Then she took out her brass kettle and shined it.

"Since this is the Fourth of July, I should do something special," she thought. "I'll use my little kettle for milking this evening."

Bossy seemed glad to see Marie when she went to the barn that evening. She mooed softly as she gave Marie a kettle full of nice warm milk.

"I'm glad you're here," Marie said to the cow. "You're company for me while everyone else is away."

Bossy began mooing strangely.

"What's the matter? Are you lonely out here in the barn all by yourself?" asked Marie. "Well, come up to the cabin with me. You can stand by the door while I get supper ready."

They started toward the cabin, Marie carrying the heavy brass kettle filled with milk and Bossy walking behind her.

Suddenly the cow mooed in a loud, shrill way. Marie turned like a flash.

There, standing near the woods, was a wolf. Marie's heart beat loud and fast. She was almost too frightened to move.

Slowly the wolf started to walk toward her. Marie remembered hearing her grandfather say that when a timber wolf comes out of the forest, he is wild and dangerous and will kill anything he sees.

She thought, too, of her father saying, "Little girls do not need guns."

Marie wanted to run into the cabin and close the door, but she did not want to leave the cow alone with the wolf.

"Dear God, please help me!" she said. Marie watched the wolf. The wild animal came closer and closer. Suddenly Marie lifted the kettle of milk and threw it right into the wolf's face. The milk spilled over his head and rolled into his eyes. The kettle fell down over his face, and the handle went under his chin.

The wolf tried and tried to get the kettle off his head. He kept backing up until he backed right into the barn. Quick as a wink, Marie closed the barn door. Then she ran into the cabin.

When her mother came home a little later, she asked, "Why isn't Bossy in the barn where she belongs?"

Marie told the story of what had happened.

Soon Marie's father and brothers came home. Jim did not win the prize.

He put his hand on Marie's shoulder and said, "I'll keep on trying to find a wolf for you."

"You'll not have to bother," said Mother. "Marie has a wolf." She told what had happened while they were away.

The boys ran to the barn and found the wolf, still trying to get rid of the kettle.

"Will you give him to me for a gun?" Jim asked his sister.

Marie shook her head as she quietly said, "No." Although it seemed strange, she no longer wanted a gun. She even wanted to keep milking Bossy.

She would use the wolf money for something else. She would have her picture made to send to her grandparents.

"I shall wear my ruffled dress, my new shawl, and my new stockings, and I shall hold my brass kettle," she said.

The six boys went on hunting, and Marie proudly learned to be a good housekeeper like other pioneer girls.

Miriam E. Mason

Off to the First Valley School

It was a cold January morning outside of the Miller family's log cabin. The ground was frozen, and there were piles of snow all around. Inside the cabin a fire burned brightly under the kettles that hung from a pole in the fireplace.

This was an exciting day for the four Miller children because today they were going to a real school for the first time.

Ted was ten years old. John and Joan were eight-year-old twins, and Kathy was seven. They were all old enough to have gone to school sooner, but there had never been a school in the valley.

Like many other pioneer mothers, Mrs. Miller had taught her children to read and write at home. Now she was glad that there would be a real school, with a real teacher, for the valley children.

"I wonder what our teacher will be like," said Joan.

"I can't imagine," answered Mrs. Miller. "I've heard that his name is Mr. Blackstone and that he moved into the valley just three days ago."

Several months before, the valley families had heard that Mr. Blackstone was willing to come and open a school. The men of the valley had built a log schoolhouse. Of course, it had only one room, and all the classes would be in that room with the same teacher.

Mrs. Miller looked carefully at the children to be sure they looked all right.

"You must hurry," she told them. "You have a long walk to school."

The children quickly put on their sweaters and coats. Mrs. Miller took some eggs from the boiling water that was in one of the kettles.

"It is very cold outside this morning," she said. "Hold these eggs in your hands, and they will help to keep you warm." She gave each child two eggs—one for each hand.

"At lunch time you can eat the eggs with your cornbread," she told them.

The children started walking through the fields with their heads down to keep the cold January wind off their faces.

91

When they reached the woods, only a gentle breeze blew, but it was dark and quiet.

"I don't want to walk through there," cried John. "It's spooky! There might be snakes, wild animals, or Indians hiding behind the trees."

"Keep still!" Ted told him. "You'll frighten the girls. Even if we did meet Indians, they would not hurt us. They're friendly around here now."

"Maybe the Indians are, but what about the wild animals?" asked John.

Just then Kathy started to scream. "What's that?" she cried.

"Now see what you have done," Ted said. "You've frightened Kathy."

When the children turned to look back at Kathy, they saw a large gray animal coming toward them.

"A wolf! It's a wolf!" screamed John and Joan.

Ted didn't have time to think what to do, but he did something. He threw his two hard-boiled eggs to the ground. He threw them so hard that they broke.

The gray animal stopped and sniffed at them. Then he started to eat the eggs. This gave Ted an idea. "Drop your eggs and run!" he shouted to the other children.

The children did as Ted said, and the animal kept on eating while they ran away. Ted helped Kathy because she was so frightened she could hardly run.

"Don't cry," he told his sister. "We're almost there."

They skated across a frozen creek. The new school was just a little past the creek, and so they kept on running.

As John, Joan, and Kathy ran toward the schoolhouse, Ted looked around and saw that the big gray animal was following them again. It came nearer and nearer and then rushed past them.

Ted saw the teacher standing in the doorway. The animal jumped on the teacher, but Mr. Blackstone just laid his hand on the animal, saying, "Down, Wolf, down!"

Then the teacher spoke to the children. "Don't be afraid," he said. "This is my dog. His name is Wolf."

"Oh, we thought he was a *real* wolf," gasped John; "not a tame dog!"

"That is easy to believe," said Mr. Blackstone. "He looks like a wolf. I'm sure he has some wolf blood in him."

"He has something else in him, too," laughed Ted, "eight hard-boiled eggs!"

Then the children told Mr. Blackstone what they had done to make the animal stop running after them.

"That was a good idea," said the teacher. "I think I am going to have a bright class to teach."

Ella Tunnell

Old Log House

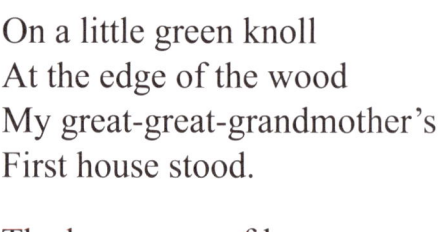

On a little green knoll
At the edge of the wood
My great-great-grandmother's
First house stood.

The house was of logs
My grandmother said
With one big room
And a lean-to shed.

The logs were cut
And the house was raised
By pioneer men
In the olden days.

They split the shingles;
They filled each chink;
It's a house of which
I like to think.

Forever and ever
I wish I could
Live in a house
At the edge of a wood.

James S. Tippett

Prayer and Praise

From their beautiful farm lands the valley folks praised God and learned about others who have given Him praise.

Cousin Lorenzo Carries the News

A Saturday Visitor

One day Cousin Lorenzo stopped at Grandma Hawkins' house. It was a cool, rainy Saturday.

Grandma already had company. Sara Lind had come over that day. She had a magazine with a picture of a sweater she wanted to make. Sara knew that Grandma Hawkins could help her get the sweater started.

Grandma had built a small fire in the fireplace. She and Sara were sitting by the fire, talking about the sweater.

Grandma looked out of the window and saw something that did not please her. She had a frown on her face.

"Here comes Cousin Lorenzo," she said.

"Oh, dear me!" said Sara. "Cousin Lorenzo will talk all morning. We won't get anything done on the sweater while he's around."

"He never knows when to go home," added Grandma.

Cousin Lorenzo knocked at Grandma Hawkins' door and smiled brightly when she opened it. "How nice and warm it is in here," he said with a cheerful voice as he closed the door behind him.

Lorenzo had a long, sharp nose like a fox. He had long, sharp whiskers just like a cat's whiskers.

"Something smells very good in here!" he said, sniffing the air with his long, sharp nose.

Lorenzo looked at Grandma's chairs and chose the most comfortable one. He put out his long legs so that his feet were close to the fire.

Cousin Lorenzo was not really Grandma Hawkins' cousin. He was not anybody's cousin. He had no family and no home of his own.

He liked being with people, and so he traveled about doing chores for some of the farmers.

Cousin Lorenzo also liked to spend his time whittling wood with his sharp knife while he talked.

"This is a good day for visiting," said Cousin Lorenzo, looking cheerful and comfortable. "I don't suppose you have any work for me on a wet day like this."

"Rain does not keep good farmers from working. They always find work to do somewhere around the farm," scolded Grandma Hawkins. "You know I have nothing for you to do. Why did you come here?"

"My father and brothers are busy today," said Sara. "They can't do much out in the rain, but they are cleaning the barn. Maybe you could help them."

Cousin Lorenzo didn't say anything, but Grandma Hawkins thought he had a strange smile on his face.

Cousin Lorenzo chose a smooth piece of wood that was in front of the fireplace. Then he opened his sharp knife and began to whittle.

"Something important is going to happen tomorrow," he said after some time.

"Now, what could be so important out here in the country?" Grandma Hawkins wanted to know.

Cousin Lorenzo went on whittling.

He always had lots of news. Since he traveled around so much, he knew everything that was going on in Honey Spring Valley.

"Do you know those two young priests with the motor chapel who are giving a mission up in the hills?" he asked.

"I do," said Sara. "I talked to them when they came through the valley."

"Well, what about them?" asked Grandma in a cross little voice. She knew that it always took Cousin Lorenzo so long to tell anything, and she was eager to hear the news.

"They are leaving tomorrow after they have their last Mass in the hill country," he said. "Father Dale thought it would be nice for some of the valley people to go up there for their last Mass."

"That would be nice," said Grandma Hawkins.

"Now, Father Dale wants me to take care of everything," Cousin Lorenzo said, pushing his chin and whiskers out proudly. "I must see that every family knows about the Mass. Then it is my job to get rides for them."

Grandma Hawkins said at once that she would like to go.

"I'm sure my mother and father will want to go," said Sara. "You can ride with us if Dad drives."

"Now, Sara," said Lorenzo suddenly, "that's my job."

Then he said to Grandma Hawkins, "I will ask Sara's parents if you can ride with them."

Then Cousin Lorenzo put away his whittling knife and said, "Well, I must get on with my work. I have to call or visit thirteen more families today."

A Proud News Carrier

Sunday morning came, and it seemed that Cousin Lorenzo had talked to many people. Nearly everyone from Holy Cross Parish was at the motor chapel for Mass.

It was a lovely morning. The sky was a heavenly blue, and the grass and trees looked greener than usual in the bright sunlight. There was no one to sing the Mass, but many little wrens chirped as they flew over the motor chapel.

As Sara knelt with her family and Grandma Hawkins she thought of what a lovely church the great outdoors makes. "After all," she thought, "this church was made by God Himself."

After Mass was over, Father Gardener thanked the people for coming. Then he said something else.

"Father Francis and I are very happy this morning," he said. "This is the largest crowd of people we have ever had at any of our Masses at the motor chapel.

"Many of you would not be here this morning if it had not been for Cousin Lorenzo."

The priest looked at the whiskered face of Lorenzo and added, "Carrying news can sometimes be very important."

Sara had never seen Cousin Lorenzo look taller or prouder.

"Why, his buttons look like they'll pop right off his coat," she whispered to Grandma Hawkins. "You may be right about Cousin Lorenzo not working as hard as other valley folks, but he truly is a good man. I'm happy that he lives in Honey Spring Valley."

"You know," said Grandma Hawkins quietly, "I'm happy for Lorenzo, too."

Blessing the Seeds

"Does anyone know what we will do tomorrow?" Sister Mary Peter asked her class at Holy Cross School one day.

Almost every hand went up. Everyone was eager to answer.

Mary Ann Brooks answered Sister's question. "Tomorrow is the day for the blessing of flowers and seeds," she said. "Father Dale will bless them and say a prayer, asking God to bless our farm lands."

"Why, I never heard of that," said Larry Long in surprise.

"I guess we learned about it while you were living in the city," said Tim Turner. "A visiting priest came here and told us about it. Father Dale, the sisters, and all the people liked the idea. Ever since then we have been bringing flowers and seeds for the blessing."

The next morning Larry and Patty Long met the other boys and girls at the school bus. Everyone had either an armful of flowers or a jar of seeds.

Jenny Hunt was carrying a small jar of seeds, but she didn't carry them for long. As Jenny was walking toward the church she fell down, and her seeds spilled beside the paved driveway.

Larry Long saw the seeds spill, and he saw the tears that began to roll down Jenny's cheeks.

"All my seeds are gone," cried Jenny.

They were very special flower seeds to Jenny. She had bought them with pennies and dimes she had saved. She had planned to plant them in her own little garden. Jenny had imagined how pretty her flowers were going to be, but now there would be no flowers.

Larry tried to help Jenny find the tiny seeds hidden in the grass, but they could find only three.

"At least, you have some seeds to take into the church for the blessing," Larry said, trying to make Jenny feel a little better. "Come on, now, or we will be late."

The unhappy girl followed Larry into the church with her few seeds.

Before Mass began, all the children and many of the grownups carried their flowers and seeds to the altar. Jenny took the few seeds that she had left. There, Father Dale blessed them.

Then he and all the people prayed this prayer:

"Almighty God, hear our prayer, and send Thy blessing upon the fields in which these seeds will be planted. Help them to grow and bear fruit. Keep them unharmed from cold, storms, and floods. Amen."

The Mass that morning was offered to beg God's special blessing upon the fields and farms of Honey Spring Valley.

On the way over to the school building Larry talked to Sister Mary Peter about how surprised he had been by the new kind of blessing.

"There is always something new going on in the valley," said Larry. "Maybe that is why we're so glad to be back."

Something that Larry didn't know about was happening right at that moment. He knew that it was raining, but he did not think that the rain was making the ground softer and that Jenny's flower seeds were sinking down into the earth.

Larry didn't even think about the seeds until one warm Sunday morning. There, growing near the church driveway where Jenny had spilled her seeds, he saw some lovely flowers.

After Mass Larry showed Jenny her beautiful flowers. Then they told Father Dale how they got there.

"You must have thought that your seeds would be useless," Father Dale said to Jenny. "But look, they have made the churchyard very lovely."

The next day Sister Mary Peter told the children about Jenny's flowers. Then she told them something else.

"Starting next spring Father Dale would like each one of you to plant a few seeds along the driveway," she said. "It will be another way to make our church grounds lovely."

"And just think!" said Larry. "It happened only because Jenny spilled her seeds."

Friend of the Farmer

A Picture for the Scrapbook

Michael Parks was in Sister Mary Peter's class at Holy Cross School. The children in his class had decided to make a scrapbook and put stories and pictures about farm life in it.

One Thursday morning Michael jumped off the bus and rushed into the classroom with the speed of a jet.

"I have a picture for our scrapbook to show you, Sister," he exclaimed.

Quick as a wink Michael opened his book bag and took out his picture.

"You know who that is, don't you, Michael?" Sister asked the excited boy.

"I do now because I read the story that was with the picture," replied Michael. "Do you suppose the other boys and girls know?"

"Let's find out if they do," whispered his teacher. "When it is time to discuss ideas for our scrapbook, you may show the picture."

Michael could hardly wait. He was sure that no one else in the class would have an idea as good as his.

In the afternoon after the spelling lesson was finished, Sister Mary Peter said, "We will take a few minutes now to discuss ideas for our scrapbook. Michael has found a very good picture for the book. Let's see who knows what the picture is about."

Very proudly Michael held up the picture for the other children to see.

"I know who that is," cried Tim.

"So do I," exclaimed Billy.

Other boys and girls in the room could have told about the picture, but they knew that Michael was proud and happy. Besides, Michael's family had always lived in the city until just a few weeks ago, and the children wanted him and his sister Barbara to like the country and everything about farm life.

"This is a picture of St. Isidore, the patron of farmers," said Michael. "I found a story about him, too. Would you like to hear it?"

"Yes, read it!" cried the children.

Michael began reading in a clear voice.

The Story of St. Isidore

Many years ago there lived, in the country of Spain, a young lad named Isidore. His parents were so poor that the lad couldn't go to school. Instead, he had to work hard and help earn a living for the family.

Isidore liked to do farm work because it helped him think about God and the wonderful gifts God has given us.

Each morning before going to work Isidore stopped in the village church to hear Mass.

One time, when he was working for a rich man who owned a large farm, Isidore stayed in church longer than usual and was late for work.

Some of the other workers told the owner of the farm about Isidore. They said he was lazy and that he left all the work for them to do.

This, of course, made the rich man angry. He went to the fields at once to see how much work Isidore had done.

"What do I see?" said the rich man to himself as he walked toward one of the fields which was being plowed. He rubbed his eyes and looked again.

Two angels with plows were walking beside Isidore. His field was plowed better than any of the others, and Isidore had finished more work than the other men.

"Angels!" exclaimed the owner, and he began to walk closer to the place where Isidore was working. When he got there, however, he saw that Isidore was alone. The angels had disappeared.

Michael finished the story by saying, "That is one of the reasons why St. Isidore has been chosen as the patron of farmers."

"That is a good story," said Larry.

"It's a good picture for our scrapbook, too," said Theresa.

Tim Turner raised his hand. "I know another story about St. Isidore," he told the class. "I read it in the *Farm News* a few months ago.

"One cold January morning in Spain St. Isidore and another man were sent to the mill with bags of wheat to be ground into flour," Tim began.

"On the way they saw a flock of hungry birds trying to find something to eat in the snow. Isidore stopped and opened his bag, for he did not like to see anyone suffering and hungry. He gave half of his wheat to the little birds.

"When the two men reached the mill, Isidore opened his bag and found that it was filled to the very top."

"That was a miracle, wasn't it?" said Carl.

"Yes, God helped Isidore because the saint had helped His poor little winged creatures," replied Sister Mary Peter.

Then she smiled and added, "God does many wonderful things on our farms every day. I wonder if any of you can name some of them."

One of the boys named the rain. Another said that God sends sunshine.

"What happens when the farmer plants a bag of wheat?" Sister asked.

"It usually grows," answered the boys and girls.

"Yes, that is right," replied Sister Mary Peter. "Did you ever stop to think that from one bag of seeds the farmer gets a whole field of wheat? Isn't that wonderful?"

The children looked surprised. They had never really thought of that before.

Soon they were discussing many other wonderful things that happen on the farm just because God loves us.

Can you think of what some of them might be?

Franz the Server

Dreams of the Fair

Here is a story that the boys and girls in Sister Mary Peter's class liked very much. It is about a little farmer boy who lived in another country long ago.

Tomorrow was the day for the fair. Tonight Franz stood in the orchard, dreaming of the joys of the fair. All his life, as long as he could remember, he had longed for the time when he would be old enough to go to the fair with his brothers. Now the time had come.

Franz pictured it all to himself as Hans and Carl had described it time and again. He would hear the noise of the band, the music of the merry-go-round, the happy voices of the people, and the children singing.

He seemed almost to smell the sugared apples, the chocolate candy, and the pleasing smell on the ladies' gowns.

He could see it too—the great colored ribbons and balloons, the painted cars and horses of the merry-go-round, the mountains of gingerbread and sugar cakes, the piles of fruit, the flashes of fairylike lights, the laughing crowd of merrymakers!

Franz had worked. He had helped his mother to milk the cows. He had carried in wheat until his arms hurt. He had gathered the fruit in heavy basketfuls for Carl. He had earned his own money to spend at the fair.

Upstairs on the bed his suit was laid out. It was his red suit with brass buttons that he wore only for great feast days. There were the new white stockings, too, that Mother had made for him last winter. Even now Hans and Carl were very busy getting the horse ready for tomorrow's trip.

They were starting at sunrise, for it was an hour's drive, which would be too much during the hot part of the day for the old horse. Besides, they must have a long day at the fair!

"Oh, tomorrow, do come!" Franz cried to the apple trees. And through the darkness, ringing very clear as sounds do by night, came the clatter of horses' hoofs over the road and up the drive to the farmhouse.

Soon a loud voice was heard calling from the farmhouse, "Franz, come here. The good priest from the village has come to speak to you."

In the farm kitchen Franz saw his father and the priest. They were sitting at a table drinking large cups of hot coffee.

Franz stood in the doorway. His heart beat fast. He knew the meaning of the priest's visit.

Invitation to a Feast

"Franz," said his father, "you are to ride back with the priest and serve Mass tomorrow. The other altar boy is ill, and there is no one to serve Mass."

It was not wise to quarrel with his father, but—tomorrow! Franz spoke in a small voice, "I am going to the fair tomorrow."

"What!" said his father. "The priest has come five miles to get you and take you back with him! No, no, Franz, get your cloak and get ready to go."

The priest could see that Franz was very disappointed. He called the boy close to him and held his hand.

"Franz need not come," he said to the boy's father. "I will get along without him."

Franz looked into the priest's face. It was pale and tired.

Franz thought the priest must have wanted an altar boy very much if he had come so far to get him.

The little boy felt unhappy. He never liked serving Mass, and just now he didn't even like the priest. He moved his body a little to show that he didn't like him, but the priest only placed his big hand over Franz' little one and smiled at him.

Franz wished that Carl could serve the Mass, but he himself had just learned the prayers. His brothers had never been taught them at all.

Franz remembered now that he had once told the priest that he would like to be a martyr. He was sure the priest was thinking of that now. It made Franz feel more uncomfortable than ever.

"I can't come with you," Franz told the priest. "I just can't. I must go to the fair. You don't understand how much I want to go to the fair!"

The priest answered softly, "Yes, Franz, I do understand. Once I, too, was looking forward to a great fair and to all the good things there. It was going to last, for what seemed to me, all my life."

Franz opened his blue eyes very wide. "Forever?" he asked.

"No, really for only one short day," answered the priest, "but to me it seemed like a long time."

"Did you go and have fun?" Franz asked.

"No, I did not go to my fair," the priest said. "I had another invitation to the great Feast the King had prepared. I answered that invitation."

Franz knew that the King was Our Lord, and now He was inviting him to come to His Feast. He bit his lips not to cry in front of the priest and his own father. He felt very, very unhappy.

"It's strange for Our Lord to send His invitations on the days of the fair," Franz said rather crossly.

The priest held the boy's hand more tightly. "It is a very big sign of His love," he said.

"I can't," said Franz.

"Very well," replied the priest. "He would not want you to come unhappily. I would not either."

The priest stood up, put on his cloak, and said good-by. He said nothing more about needing a Mass server.

The priest had started riding off down the road when suddenly Franz ran after him and caught up with him. He looked up at the priest in the darkness and said, "I want to come with you."

After his long ride through the night air, Franz slept deeply. Just before sunrise the boy sleepily got out of his bed and started getting dressed. Franz wondered why he had such a strange feeling. It was just as if there were a lot of strings tangled around his heart.

As Franz looked out over the fields and saw the little red clouds riding up in the sky, he remembered. Just now Carl and Hans were getting out the horse, or perhaps they had already started off for the fair.

Feast of the King

Heavy hearted, Franz followed the priest to a small church. He lighted the candles. How small and dim they looked as Franz thought of the bright lights at the fair!

"In the name of the Father and of the Son and of the Holy Spirit," the priest began. "I will go to the altar of God. To God, Who gives joy. . . ."

The prayers of the Mass went on. Now the priest was asking God's forgiveness for sins. As Franz said his part of the prayer for forgiveness with his lips, his thoughts were with Carl and Hans.

"I wonder if they are riding the merry-go-round now," he thought.

"The Lord be with you," said the priest.

Suddenly Franz hoped the Lord would really be with him, for he was very much afraid that a tear would fall.

"I'm not crying," he told himself. "And with thy spirit," he answered the priest.

The Mass went on, and through the server's head the thought of everything at the fair went on at the same time.

Suddenly Franz shook himself and looked at the altar. The priest was lifting the paten. Franz knew that the little host was on the paten.

He remembered that he should offer himself with the host, and for the first time he realized that he could do that.

"I came to Your Feast, Almighty God, instead of going to the fair," he said. "I didn't want to, but I'm glad I did."

Then he realized that there was no one else in the church hearing the Mass. He wondered if everyone was at the fair.

It seemed strange that he, Franz, who longed to be somewhere else, should be the only one at the King's Sacred Feast. It would be unkind not to enjoy the Holy Feast. It almost seemed as if it was prepared only for him.

Then he straightened his shoulders and began to smile. "I'm smiling," he said to God. He was beginning to be really glad that he was there. He felt sorry for the King Who had no one but himself at His Feast. The very thought made him forget to be sorry for himself.

Franz was holding the water and wine, and the tear he had been trying to keep back rolled down his cheek and fell into the water. The priest seemed not to see it, but Franz saw the tear gleaming in the chalice like a diamond in the wine.

As he turned to put the water and wine back on the table he saw something very strange. Just for a moment it seemed as if there was a large crowd of people in the church, more than he had ever seen. They were all looking at the chalice which the priest was holding up.

The people were not all of his own country. Some were rich; some, poor. Some were dark-skinned, and some wore clothes like those of olden times. And every one of them had a tear on his cheek and a smile on his lips.

Franz turned back toward the altar. The golden chalice, in which he knew his tear was shining like a diamond, was covered now.

As he looked at it he felt as if a flock of birds had broken into song in his heart. They all seemed to be singing the words the priest was saying, "Come, Almighty and eternal God, and bless this sacrifice which is prepared for the glory of Thy holy name."

Franz lifted his face, and he knew that a great crowd lifted their hearts with his. Franz the server lifted not only his soul to God, but also the heart of Christ, for Christ lives in the hearts of the faithful.

Later at the Consecration of the Mass, the priest lifted the chalice. When he said the words of Consecration, it was then that Franz saw his tear turn red and disappear. It was then that he knew the tear to be all the sacrifice and sorrow of the world. He knew that it was no longer a boy's tear that had spilled into the water, but the Blood of Christ Himself.

That day Our Lord gave Franz his second invitation to His Feast. He received it this time not with tears, but with glory and joy in his heart.

Although he had many years to wait, when the time came, Franz went eagerly from the fair of life to the Feast of God.

Caryll Houselander

Blessed Be God

Blessed be God for the little birds,
   Blessed be God for the sky,
Blessed be God for the billowy clouds
   That swiftly go sailing by.

Blessed be God for the pretty flowers,
   Blessed be God for the ground,
Blessed be God for the rain and the sun
   And shady trees we have found.

Blessed be God for the summertime,
   Blessed be God for the spring,
Blessed be God for the beautiful world.
   To Him our praise we sing.

Sister Rose Margaret, C.S.J.

Here Comes the Bookmobile

Every month a bookmobile brought library books with wonderful stories to the valley. Here are some stories that the children liked best.

The Queen Bee

There was once a king who had three sons. The two older ones went out into the world to make their fortunes. They were lazy boys, and instead of making a fortune, they soon lost all of their money and could not return home.

After some time, the youngest son decided that he would go out and look for his two brothers. One day as he wandered through the woods he found them.

"I have come to travel with you and to make my fortune, too," he told them.

"Nonsense!" laughed the two older brothers. "You're too silly and stupid to do anything. We are older and wiser, but we have not been able to get along in the world."

The youngest brother refused to go home, so the two boys took him along.

As they were walking through some tangled bushes in the woods they came upon a large ant hill. The two older brothers wanted to hit it and knock it down. They thought it would be fun to watch the ants run away in fright.

"No, let the poor things enjoy their life," said the youngest boy, stepping forward to pull his brothers away from the ant hill.

On the three brothers went. Soon they came to a sparkling clear lake where many ducks were swimming.

The two older brothers wanted to shoot two of the ducks and roast them.

Again the youngest brother begged, "Leave the poor ducks alone. Do not kill them."

The brothers walked away. They were still scolding the youngest lad for not letting them have fun, when they came upon a bee's nest in a tree. The nest was so full of honey that it ran down the side of the tree.

"Ah, honey!" cried one of the brothers. "Let's build a fire and smoke out the bees. Then we can have all the honey that we can eat."

"Oh, please don't do that," begged the youngest lad. "Let the poor bees live and enjoy their nest."

Toward evening the three brothers came to a palace that was very quiet. There seemed to be no one around. They walked into one of the barns where they saw about fifty fine horses and ponies, but they were all of marble.

They walked through the gardens, but they did not see one living man, woman, child, or animal.

Since the door of the palace stood wide open, they walked inside. They went from one room to another without meeting anyone. Finally, in one room they saw a little old man.

"Good evening, sir!" they called to him. The man did not move. They shouted louder. Three times they called.

At last the old man seemed to hear. He walked toward the three boys, but not one word did he say. He took them to a table covered with all kinds of delicious foods. After the brothers had a wonderful meal, the little old man showed them into a beautiful bedroom where they slept.

The next morning the little man took the oldest boy to a large hall where there were three smooth marble tablets. The writing on the tablets told of the palace enchantment and how the enchantment could be broken.

The first tablet said, "In the woods hidden under some bushes and weeds, there are one thousand diamonds which belong to the princesses. All of these must be found before sundown. If only one is missing, he who is looking for the diamonds will be changed into marble."

The oldest brother thought this was easy enough to do, so he set out to find the diamonds. All day long he hunted through the tangled bushes and weeds. By sundown he had not even found one hundred diamonds, and so he was changed at once into a marble statue.

The next day the second brother tried to find the thousand diamonds, but he also failed and was turned to marble.

On the third day, the youngest brother tried his luck. He was almost ready to give up when five thousand ants came forward. They were the ones whose lives he had saved.

The ants tore through the patches of weeds with great speed, and before the sun started to sink, they had found all the gleaming diamonds. They piled them before the boy.

When he took them back to the palace, the little old man showed him the second marble tablet. On the tablet it said, "The key to the bedroom of the princesses must be found. It is at the bottom of the lake. If it is not found by sundown, he who has tried and failed will be turned into marble."

The youngest boy stood at the edge of the lake wondering how to get the key. While he was thinking, two ducks came forward. They were the same ones whose lives he had saved some days before.

The two ducks then disappeared under the water, found the key in the mud at the bottom of the lake, and brought it to the young lad.

"How lucky I am," the boy thought, but he had one more thing to do before the enchantment could be broken.

The old man showed the lad a third tablet. On it were these words, "The king's three daughters all have eaten something sweet. The oldest had a piece of sugar candy, the second one had some maple syrup, and the youngest had honey. You must choose the one who has eaten the honey."

The youngest lad looked at the three marble statues and frowned. All three princesses looked just alike.

"Oh, my!" thought the young lad. "How shall I ever be able to choose the youngest when they all look alike?"

He felt worried and frightened. Then into the hall flew the queen bee whose nest he had saved a few days before. The queen bee's flight stopped when she came to the marble statues.

She sat on the pale mouth of one of the princesses, and the lad knew that this was the princess who had eaten honey.

At that very minute the enchantment was broken. Everything in the palace came back to life. The king and queen began to move. The princesses laughed and danced. The birds chirped, and the dogs barked.

Everyone was happy, but the youngest princess and the youngest brother were the happiest of them all. They were married the next day and lived happily ever after.

Retold from Grimm

The Wonderful Fortunes of a Woodcutter

In the old days many, many years ago, there lived a woodcutter and his wife. Although they were very poor and had no children, they lived happily together.

Everything went fine for the hard-working woodcutter and his wife before the day a peddler came by and told them a wonderful fairy tale. He told them how a fairy had granted a very poor man's wish and how the man had become a rich and powerful king.

The next day, for some reason or other, the woodcutter and his wife could not get their work done. They kept thinking of the peddler's wonderful tale.

Finally, the woodcutter went out into the forest. Instead of working as he did on other days, he sat wishing that a fairy would come to visit him.

Suddenly a large white rabbit stood in front of him and said in a very small voice, "Well, what can I do for you today?"

"Do for me!" exclaimed the surprised woodcutter. "What are you able to do?"

"You'd be surprised," answered the rabbit. "If I like, I can tell you where the wonderful wishing skin lies. The fairies have just finished making it. The one who is lucky enough to get it will only have to put it on, and every wish he makes will be granted at once."

The woodcutter could hardly believe his ears. Was this a magic rabbit speaking?

"There is only one bad thing about the wishing skin," the rabbit said. "It is made of wishes, you see. Every time a wish is made, the skin and the person wearing it become smaller."

"Oh, Rabbit, do you know where that fairy skin is?" asked the woodcutter.

"I know exactly where it is," replied the rabbit. "The fairies have hidden it under the old oak tree near my home."

Off ran the rabbit. Soon he was back with the wonderful skin.

"Please let me put it on and make only one wish," begged the woodcutter.

As he was putting on the skin he said, "Oh, I wish this skin were mine and I would never have to take it off."

No sooner had he said these words than the skin became smaller.

"Oh, my!" exclaimed the rabbit. "Why did you say that? Your new skin has already grown smaller. Please take the skin off and give it back to me, or the fairies may punish me for taking it away."

The woodcutter knew that his wish had been granted because he could not take the skin off.

The poor rabbit begged and begged until the woodcutter could stand it no longer and said, "I wish you would be carried to the other end of the world."

At once his wish was granted, and the rabbit disappeared.

As soon as the woodcutter reached home he made another wish. "I wish we had onion soup, roast beef, wine, and many servants," he said.

Quick as a flash everything appeared, but at the same time the woodcutter grew smaller. When he sat in a chair, his feet no longer reached the floor.

Later the woodcutter said, "I wish I were a rich king and had a palace and golden dishes to eat from and golden beds to sleep on."

As usual, the wish was granted, but the woodcutter became smaller than ever. Yet, he was very proud because he was dressed as a king.

When people saw the tiny man in king's robes, they laughed and laughed. Still the foolish man was not satisfied. He kept right on making wishes and getting smaller.

Finally, he became so tiny that when his wife wanted to talk to him, she had to put him on top of a table so she could see him. The servants carried him around in their hands just as if he were a toy.

Soon the king became very, very unhappy. He was not safe any place. He was always afraid that someone would step on him.

Even when he went out into the fields, he had to ring a bell. He did this so that the birds would not think he was something good to eat and carry him off to their nests.

"Oh, dear!" said the dissatisfied king, walking through the fields one nice day, "how I wish I were a strong woodcutter once again, a real man who could do hard work!"

As he said these words he stamped his foot and threw his crown to the ground. At once he felt himself growing.

Soon he was a tall, strong man again.

The woodcutter hurried to show his wife what had happened. The palace was gone, all the servants had disappeared, and his wife was just a poor woman in a little cottage.

"Now we can be happy again," she cried when she saw her husband.

Hungarian Folk Tale

The Princesses and Happy Village
The Unhappy Princesses

One beautiful spring morning three young princesses, Maybell, Marjory, and Marigold, were sitting in the lovely palace garden. They were not thinking of all the lovely things around them. They were very deep in thought about something else.

"The grand ball to be given by King James is exactly one month away," sighed Marjory very sadly. "Not one prince has invited us."

"Mother will make us go," said Maybell, "but what fun will it be? We will do nothing except sit around the wall all evening long and have no one to dance with."

"I suppose, if we were not so homely, a lot of young men would want to dance with us," added Marigold crossly.

"Last evening," said Maybell, "I heard Lady Maria telling someone that we are so homely that nothing can be done about it. She said that beauty is only skin deep, but that ugliness goes right through to the bone."

Marjory screamed, "It's terrible to be as homely as we are!"

After a few minutes a young girl carrying a basket walked into the garden. She was one of the prettiest girls the princesses had ever seen.

"What are you doing here, and what do you want?" Maybell asked in a very unpleasant manner.

"How did you get into this garden?" scolded Marjory.

"I am Elizabeth, daughter of the baker of Happy Village," replied the girl. "The guards at the gate let me through when I told them I had a gift for you."

She lifted the white cloth that covered her basket and showed a beautiful cake covered with white frosting. There were flowers and bluebirds on the cake, too.

"My father has just found a new secret way to make wedding cakes," said the girl. "He wishes to give each of you a cake like this when you are married."

"Well, you can return home and tell your father to keep his wedding cakes," Marigold said in a cross manner. "We'll never get married."

"Young men don't like homely girls—even princesses," said Marjory.

Maybell looked at Elizabeth as she asked, "Do you have many friends?"

"Oh, yes. Everyone in Happy Village has friends," answered the girl.

"I suppose that is because everyone in your village is beautiful," snapped Marjory.

"I really can't say that," replied Elizabeth, "but I do know that everyone in our village is happy. Now I must return home and help my father."

Later Marigold said, "I wonder if all the girls in Happy Village are as pretty as the baker's daughter."

"Why don't we go and find out?" asked Maybell.

The Secret of Happiness

After lunch that day the princesses asked a driver to bring the coach to the front of the palace. It was a gold coach drawn by four white horses.

"We wish to go to Happy Village," Marjory told the driver.

"Happy Village?" said the driver of the coach. "I don't know where that is."

"You certainly are very stupid," said Maybell. "Just drive on and ask the first person you meet."

Soon they met an old man. "Forgive me, sir," the driver said to him. "Do you know the way to Happy Village?"

"Why, yes," replied the man. "Go on down the road, and turn south toward the river."

Marigold looked at the old man and asked, "Is it true that all the girls in Happy Village are beautiful?"

"Yes," smiled the old man. "I guess they are beautiful because they are happy, and they are happy because they are very kind. They are always doing something to help others."

"That sounds silly and stupid to me," said Marigold, "but at least we should go and find out for ourselves."

When their coach arrived at Happy Village, Maybell said, "Let's go to the baker's shop. Maybe he can answer all our questions."

They had no trouble finding the shop.

"We wish to be beautiful," Marjory told the baker as soon as they got inside.

"We want to have many friends," said Marigold.

"An old man told us that when people do kind things for others, they are happy and beautiful," said Maybell.

"Now, I'm not sure that I know what you're talking about," replied the baker, "but if you are interested in doing something for others, I can help you."

He showed Marigold a pan of chocolate cakes. "If you want to be helpful, you can finish frosting these cakes," he said.

He told Maybell to go up the street and take care of a poor old woman who could not walk any more.

He told Marjory to take care of a little baby while the mother sewed and made clothes for her other children.

The three princesses stood looking at one another. This didn't sound very interesting to them. Since they had come so far, they decided they might just as well do what the baker had told them.

The sun was sinking down in the west when the three princesses met near the baker's shop to go back to their palace.

"Why, we're just as homely as ever," they said, looking at each other.

"It was a stupid thing to do," said Maybell in a disappointed voice.

"I knew it would never work," cried Marjory.

"Maybe it didn't make us beautiful," said Marigold, "but somehow I feel different inside. It's something I never felt before. You know, it was really fun frosting those little cakes."

"I enjoyed taking care of that dear little baby," said Marjory.

"I feel different, too," said Maybell.

"Let's come back and do some more things tomorrow," said Marigold. "It's really more fun than we thought it would be."

Then every day for over a week the princesses went back to Happy Village and did things for others. They were so busy that they no longer had time to scold and be cross or to think of their clothes and how they looked.

Then, finally, the night of the grand ball came. The three princesses had to go because their parents said so. They had beautiful new gowns which their mother had brought them from Spain.

Before they left the palace, they looked at themselves in the mirror. They were so surprised that they could hardly believe their own eyes.

"Why, we're beautiful!" all three of them said as they stood before the mirror.

At the ball all the young princes wanted to dance with the three lovely princesses.

As the queen watched her daughters she said to her husband, "Our daughters are lovely in their new gowns. It's wonderful how a little color can make girls beautiful."

The princesses heard their mother, but they said nothing. They only looked at one another in a knowing way.

"It is not the clothes we are wearing," said Marigold thoughtfully.

"No, it's because we tried to be kind to others, and that made us happy. Being happy has made us beautiful," said Maybell.

"Now the baker can make those pretty wedding cakes for us after all," added Marjory. "I hope we'll never be homely again."

From that day on, the three princesses were the most beautiful and the happiest young ladies in the land.

Do you know why?

Kay Smith

Nail Soup

Late one night a beggar was walking through the forest of fir trees. He was hoping to find a place to stay when he suddenly saw lights through the trees.

Soon he saw a cottage. He went to the porch and knocked on the door.

"Good evening, and where do you come from?" asked an old man and his wife as they opened the door.

"South of the sun and east of the moon," answered the beggar. "I'm looking for a place to stay tonight."

"Well, you might just as well go on your way," said the old man, "because we don't have room for you."

"Now, my good people," said the stranger, "don't be so hardhearted. We must learn to help one another."

"Just how could you help anybody?" asked the woman.

The beggar did not move. "Won't you please just let me sleep on the floor?" he asked. He kept on begging until finally the two old folks allowed him to come in.

When he got inside the cottage, he realized the people were not as badly off as they tried to make him believe. He found out that they were greedy and never satisfied with anything.

When the beggar asked for something to eat, the old woman exclaimed, "Now, where in the world am I to get you something to eat? We haven't tasted food for over a week."

The stranger was a clever fellow, and he said, "You poor things! I'll have to ask you to share something with me."

"You don't look as if you have anything to share," scolded the old man.

"Just do me one favor," said the beggar. "Give me a kettle."

By this time the little old woman had become interested. She took out a kettle and gave it to the beggar. He filled it with water and hung it by its handle on the pole in the fireplace. Later he took a nail from his pocket and dropped it into the boiling water. The little old woman took a seat and just stared at the beggar.

"What are you making?" she asked. "Nail soup," said the beggar.

"Nail soup!" exclaimed the woman. "I've never heard of such a thing."

"Just watch me and you'll learn all about it," said the beggar.

"This usually makes good soup, but today it is a little thin," said the beggar. "I've been using this nail for a month. If we can't have dumplings in it, a handful of flour would help. Of course, since you don't have anything in the house, we'll have to forget about it."

The little old woman got up. "I may have a wee bit of flour," she said.

She went into another room and came back with a cup of flour.

"This soup would be good enough for company if only we had a little beef bone and a few potatoes to add to it," said the beggar, enjoying his little game. "Of course, since you don't have any meat, we'll have to get along without it."

The old woman got up again. She remembered that she had some beef and a few potatoes too. These she gave to the beggar as he kept stirring the soup.

The old woman watched until her eyes almost popped out of her head.

The beggar tasted the soup and said, "You know, this is grand enough to offer to a king."

"Well, I never!" said the old man. "And to think it's all from a nail! It is as if this beggar had a magic wand."

"A little milk would give it a finer taste," said the beggar, "but what one doesn't have, one must do without."

The old woman said, "I think maybe our cow can give us a little milk." She went to the barn to get it.

The beggar kept on stirring, and the old woman kept on watching. Then all at once he took the nail out of the kettle.

"Now it is ready," he said as he stopped stirring the soup. "Of course, if the king and queen were here to eat it with us, they would have some bread and wine. There would be a nice white cloth on the table. Of course, what one doesn't have, one must get along without."

By this time the old woman began to feel like a queen. She went straight to the closet and brought out her best candles, a bottle of wine, some bread, and butter and placed them on the table.

Never in all their lives had the old folks had such a grand feast. Never before had they tasted such delicious soup. Just think of it, it was made from a nail!

They even offered the beggar their best room for the night. The next morning the woman had a big pot of coffee and a dish of oatmeal ready for him.

When the beggar had finished eating the oatmeal and drinking his coffee, he started to leave the cottage.

The old people thanked him. "Now we shall always live well because we know how to make nail soup," the old woman said.

"It's not hard to make if you know what to add," replied the beggar.

"Clever fellows like that do not grow on trees," said the two old folks as they waved good-bye to the beggar.

Swedish Folk Tale

The Princess Who Could Not Cry

There was once a princess who could not cry, but that was not so bad. The real trouble was that she laughed at everything, even when it was not nice to laugh. Her parents had tried to make her stop laughing, but they could not.

"If the princess could be made to cry only once," said a wise old woman from the east, "the spell would be broken. Then she would laugh only when she should."

The king and queen offered five hundred pieces of silver to anyone who could break the spell and make the princess cry.

Wise men from all over the kingdom came to see what they could do, but not one of them made the little girl cry.

One of the wise men said that the child should be left in her bedroom and be given nothing but bread and water for a whole week.

This seemed very cruel to the queen. She was willing to try, but she allowed the princess to have bread and milk instead of bread and water.

Every time the head servant took the bread and milk to the princess, he found her spinning around happily and laughing as if she were at a party. At the end of the week she was still very cheerful.

"Look!" she exclaimed when her mother came into the room. "My feet have become so thin that I can kick my shoes off." She kicked her foot up and sent her shoe flying across the room.

The poor queen hurried to the kitchen and told the cook to see that the princess had chicken soup, ice cream, and puffy pink cake for lunch. That made the little girl laugh harder than ever.

After some time another wise man came to the palace. He had learned to make terrible noises and ugly faces. He was sure he could make the princess cry.

The king and queen waited outside the door while the wise man went in to frighten the princess. Soon loud sounds of laughter popped from the room.

The wise man opened the door and walked out. His face was red and very hot. "I've tried everything I know," he said. "I give up, for it's no use to try to make that girl cry."

The princess came running out to her parents saying, "Oh, you should have seen that silly man! He is even funnier than the funniest clowns and monkeys. He made the funniest faces I have ever seen." Then her laughter could be heard throughout the palace.

Later one wise man after another tried to break the spell, but not one of them could do it.

Now, in a small village in the same kingdom, there was a girl named Rosebud. She lived alone with her sick mother in a little cottage. Her mother needed a good doctor and medicine, but they had no money for these things.

Rosebud had heard about the princess who could not cry. Then one day while Rosebud was getting lunch ready she thought of something that would bring tears to the princess's eyes.

As soon as lunch was over Rosebud put on her hat and coat and started off for the palace carrying a little basket. Her mother tried to make her give up her idea, but the little girl was sure she could do what all the wise men had failed to do.

When she got to the palace gate, a guard came out.

"We have no food to give away today," the guard snapped.

Now, the queen heard the guard. So she came to the gate to see what Rosebud wanted. "What is it, my child?" she asked in a pleasant voice.

"Oh, Your Majesty," said Rosebud, "I've come to make the princess cry."

When the queen heard this, she shook her head and smiled. She wondered how a little country girl could do what wise men had failed to do. Rosebud begged so hard that the queen finally said she could try.

Rosebud was led into the princess's room. Of course, the princess was very happy to see the little girl, and she danced around in delight.

Within a short time news went around the palace that a little country girl was trying to make the princess cry.

"How silly and stupid!" said everyone. "She's only a child!"

Now, the king and the queen could not wait to see what was happening in the princess's room, and so they opened the door and looked in. What do you think they saw?

Their daughter was sitting quietly in her room with Rosebud's basket near her. She was peeling onions as fast as she could. As she peeled them, tears were streaming down her face.

Now, if you have ever peeled onions, you know why the princess cried.

The king and queen were so happy to see the tears that they rushed in and kissed the princess.

All the maids and servants and all the fine ladies-in-waiting stood by holding their noses. The head cook at the bottom of the stairs snapped in a cross voice, "I could have done that myself."

The good news went out all over the kingdom, and a great festival was held. At last the princess could laugh and cry like everyone else.

Rosebud received the five hundred pieces of silver. Her mother could then have the food and medicine she needed.

Indeed, the king and queen were so pleased that they invited Rosebud to the palace to play with their daughter. They showered her with all kinds of presents.

When Rosebud grew up, she married a prince, and they had onions for dinner on their wedding day.

Rose Fyleman

Crom Duv's Sunday

There is a certain day, the last Sunday in July, when large crowds of people go to a certain mountain in Ireland. A great festival is held on the same day. This is called Crom Duv's Sunday. The reason it is so named is because of something that happened there long ago.

St. Patrick, the patron saint of Ireland, was much loved during his lifetime even by all those who had not yet become Christians. He was the friend of all men.

So it came about that a great chief, called Crom Duv, wished to send a present to the saint.

The chief had just killed an ox and had cut it into four quarters. He sent one quarter of it with his greetings to St. Patrick by his errand boy.

When the boy arrived at the place where St. Patrick lived with his friends, he found the holy man in prayer. The boy waited until the saint came out, and then he presented the gift.

Now, at that time there was very little food in Ireland. Meat was never seen except on the tables of the rich because it cost so much. Indeed, St. Patrick and his friends were often hungry. Most of their food came from kind folks who lived nearby.

For this reason, when the saint saw the large piece of meat which Crom Duv had sent, he raised his eyes to heaven. Blessing the meat, he said, "Deo Gratias," which means, "Thanks be to God."

The errand boy, seeing the size of Crom Duv's gift, waited for more thanks than just two words. None came, for St. Patrick had returned to his prayers.

The boy went back to his chief, who at once asked what thanks the saint had given for the present.

"Well, now," replied the boy, "it was not more than two words. I do not know what the words mean because I have never before heard them. It's little enough thanks to bring you for such a large piece of meat—enough to feed at least twelve hungry men, so it was."

"I only get two words of thanks for a quarter of an ox!" cried Crom Duv angrily. "Maybe this Patrick thought my gift was too small. Go back with one more quarter of the ox. Say it is another gift from me, Crom Duv, chief of the land. Then come back quickly, and tell me what he said."

The boy carried another quarter of the ox and dropped it at the feet of St. Patrick where he sat under a tree, reading from his prayer book.

When the saint saw the boy with another large piece of meat, he was very pleased because he had given the first gift to the poor. Again the good saint blessed the gift, saying, "Deo Gratias."

The errand boy, afraid to go back to Crom Duv with only this short message of thanks, waited for more. Again, nothing came. So the boy had to return and tell the chief what had happened.

"Deo Gratias!" shouted Crom Duv. "Even if I knew what the words meant, they would still be poor thanks for such a grand gift. I shall try this Patrick just once more. If he does not show better thanks for my presents, I shall know what to do with him."

Again the boy was sent, carrying another quarter of the ox. He found St. Patrick listening to the song of birds.

Placing the third quarter of the ox before the saint, the errand boy waited for what he felt must be a fine message of thanks. Again he got only the two words, "Deo Gratias."

Not another sound came from St. Patrick, but his face, as he listened to the song of the birds, was very kind and gentle.

The boy had to go back, knowing very well what trouble would come from St. Patrick's short message.

"Well, what kind of thanks do you bring me this time?" growled Crom Duv, his hand upon his sword.

"Ah, now, my chief," cried the boy, looking at the sword. "Is it my mistake that the man can speak only two words? He said, 'Deo Gratias!' the first time. He said, 'Deo Gratias!' the second time. Even for the third quarter of the ox you sent him, he said, 'Deo Gratias!' again."

"And he is said to be the greatest speaker in all Ireland!" shouted Crom Duv in anger. "How could he treat me this way? Is it to say that I am not important that he throws back two words for three quarters of an ox? Run, boy, and tell Patrick that Crom Duv, chief of the land, wishes to see him at once!"

The boy ran, seeing the horrible anger in his chief's eye.

After the boy gave St. Patrick the message from Crum Duv, he said, "I beg of you to come quickly, for the chief is very angry."

"Why should your chief be angry?" asked the saint. "Has he not all things but one—the greatest of all? This, I am ready to give him!"

St. Patrick went willingly to see the chief. Even the angry look and ready sword of Crom Duv did not frighten the good man.

"You sent for me?" Patrick asked quietly.

Crom Duv shouted out angrily, "What kind of thanks have you shown me for the three quarters of a fine ox that I sent you?"

"Very deep-felt thanks," replied the saint in the same quiet voice.

"Only two words of thanks! And those words I did not understand," stormed the chief in anger.

"Those two words carried my very best thanks," explained St. Patrick. "I could not have sent you thanks in a finer way."

"Do you know how much the meat that I sent you weighed?" cried Crom Duv fiercely.

"Do you know what my thanks weighed?" asked the saint, not angry at all. "Do you have any scales, Crom Duv?"

"I have," replied Crom Duv.

"Have you also three quarters of an ox that weigh the same as the three you sent me?" asked the saint calmly.

"I have," was the fierce answer.

"Then let them be brought out," said St. Patrick.

The saint wrote the words, "Deo Gratias," three times on a piece of paper.

"Now," the saint said calmly when the meat and scales were before him, "place the three quarters of the ox on one side of the scales. On the other side I will put this paper. We shall then know which was the greater—your gift or my thanks."

Very eagerly Crom Duv watched the weighing of the meat and the paper. When the paper brought the scales right down, all the anger left the chief's face. In its place came a look of wonder.

Falling upon his knees before the saint, Crom Duv cried, "Oh, most blessed and holy Patrick! Tell me the meaning of those two words which, on only a scrap of paper, weigh more than my gift of three quarters of an ox."

"My friend," said St. Patrick, "those two words are forever blessed. 'Deo Gratias' means 'Thanks be to God.'"

Crom Duv then became a Christian. He and all his people were baptized into the Christian faith by St. Patrick, the patron saint of Ireland.

From that day, the last Sunday of July has always been known in those parts of Ireland as Crom Duv's Sunday.

Retold by E. Lucia Turnbull

Friendly Farmer Folks

There is a lot of work to be done in the country and many interesting things to learn about farm life.

The 4-H Club

One rainy afternoon Mary Ann Brooks was in her bedroom, reading a story in a farm magazine. Suddenly Andrew called her.

"Come and see what's on TV," he said. "It's about the boy who won first prize at the state fair."

Quickly Mary Ann ran downstairs.

"Look at that!" exclaimed Andrew. "That boy is only twelve years old, and he won the first prize."

Mary Ann saw a boy standing proudly in front of a big tent with his calf. There was a blue ribbon on the calf.

"It looks as if the calf won," laughed Mary Ann. "She has the ribbon." "Listen!" said her brother.

The boy on TV told how he raised the calf by himself. He had learned to do it through the 4-H Club.

After that there were pictures taken inside the big tent of many other farm boys and girls who had learned to do interesting things through the 4-H Club.

Some of the boys were raising calves. They were also raising other animals and vegetables. Some of the girls were cooking, sewing, and canning foods.

"It all sounds like a lot of extra chores to me," said Mary Ann. She thought for a moment and added, "Maybe the four H's stand for housework, hayfields, horses, and hens."

"That's clever," Andrew said, "but it's not right. The four H's mean head, health, heart, and hands."

The two children stopped talking and listened carefully when they heard the man on the TV program say something about a 4-H Club starting in the valley.

"Mr. Jack Long will be the leader," the man said. "All those wishing to become members should talk to him."

"That's great!" exclaimed Andrew. "I'm sure Dad will let me join. I'll be eleven years old next month."

"Can't I join?" asked his sister.

"No, you're only eight years old, and you must be ten to be a member of the 4-H Club," replied her brother.

"I'm tall," said Mary Ann. "Maybe I could say I'm ten."

"Not unless you want to tell a lie," said Andrew. "If you tell lies, you will not be a very good club member."

News of a 4-H Club in the valley got around very fast. Then one day Mr. Long called a meeting of all those who had signed up and wanted to belong.

"The club will give you your first calf, pig, or sheep, and you must take care of it," he told them.

Each of the twelve members was allowed to choose what he wished to do.

"I want to raise calves," said Tim.

"I'll begin with sheep," said Andrew. "Dad says the rough pasture behind our barn will be good for sheep."

Billy's older brother had read a book about taking care of fruit trees, and he decided to raise peaches.

Each member was interested in one thing or another, but all were interested in making farm life happier and better.

Before the meeting closed, the boys and girls decided to name their club "The Happy Honeys."

The next week Mr. Long took all the new 4-H Club members to Leesburg for an important meeting. It was a meeting of all the 4-H Clubs and their leaders from all over the county.

A man from one of the county schools near Leesburg talked to the boys and girls about farm life and farm work.

"When farmers work together and help one another, instead of trying to do everything alone, they have an easier job," he said.

The boys and girls listened to another speaker. He had an office in Leesburg and was called the county agent.

"If you have any problems with your work, you must come to the county agent's office for help," he said.

"The county agent can tell you what medicines to give sick animals. He can tell you when different vegetables should be sprayed. He will also tell you how to raise healthy farm animals."

The children were surprised to learn that the county agent was so interested in the members of the 4-H Clubs.

Tim thought of the time when many of his mother's chickens had become sick and died.

"If we had known about the work of the county agent's office at that time, perhaps the chickens could have been saved," he thought.

When the meeting was over, the Happy Honeys said good-by to their new friends. They also promised to work hard at their special kinds of farm work.

The Bicycle Tree
Waiting for Peaches

Carl Singer leaned against the fence and stared at his peach tree, but without really seeing it. Instead, he was seeing his bright red bicycle.

If he squinted his eyes just right, all the branches of the tree seemed to twist themselves around until the tree looked like a big new bicycle for Carl.

To be sure, the bicycle was not red yet, but it was going to be the reddest bicycle in the county when he got busy with a paint can. It wasn't his own yet, either, but it was going to be.

"If you do your part," Carl told the peach tree. The tree said nothing at all, but only stood there looking beautiful in its spring dress of soft pink.

"What are you doing, Carl?" asked. Betty, his baby sister, perched on the fence beside him.

"Looking at my bicycle tree," Carl answered.

Betty laughed and asked, "Does it grow bicycles?"

"Sort of," said Carl. "Pretty soon that tree will have some peaches on it, and then I'll pick the peaches and sell them. If I get five dollars worth, I'll be riding my own bicycle to school in the fall."

Carl was thinking how lucky he was that the Big Brothers' Bicycle was ready for him. His biggest brother had bought it six years ago for twenty-five dollars. Three years later he sold it for twenty dollars to Carl's second-from-top brother, Freddy. Now Freddy was going to sell it to Carl for ten dollars, as soon as Carl got the ten dollars.

In his red-and-white pig bank, Carl had exactly five dollars.

"Dad said that my tree would have at least two bushels of peaches," said Carl. "Even if some of the peaches are bad, I should get five dollars."

"When do the peaches come?" asked Betty, who was too little to remember back to last year.

"Pretty soon," said Carl.

"May I help pick them?" Betty asked.

"Oh, sure," said Carl, trying to count the blossoms on the tree, but he couldn't count even those on one branch.

Carl knew that every blossom meant a peach or a maybe-peach.

After the blossoms died and fell, nothing happened for what seemed like a very long time to Carl. He did earn another seventy-five cents cutting grass and bought a can of bright red paint to paint the bicycle with as soon as it was his.

Finally, one day when he went out, Dad was going up and down the orchard, sending clouds of white spray over all the trees.

Carl hurried to his tree, and there the peaches were, tiny and green.

Betty reached out a finger and touched one. "Let's pick them now," she said, "so you can get your bicycle."

"Not yet," said Carl. "They have to be a whole lot bigger."

In another two weeks some of the peaches dropped off and fell on the ground.

"Now we can sell some," said Betty.

"No," Carl laughed. "Those fall off because they aren't any good or because there are more than the tree can feed. They call that the June drop."

Just to make sure that this was still his bicycle tree, Carl looked up and squinted. Sure enough, the branches twisted around into something that looked exactly like a bicycle for Carl. Before very long it was July, and the peaches were growing bigger every day.

No More Waiting

"I'm going to have plenty of money for the bicycle," said Carl to himself.

One day as he looked down through the orchard, he could see Betty's pink dress by his peach tree. Walking toward the tree, Carl called to his sister.

And then he stopped, with his mouth wide open and his heart going down to the bottom of his boots. He couldn't see a single peach on the bicycle tree!

Instead, a bushel basket was sitting under the tree, full of hard, green peaches that wouldn't have been ripe for another six weeks.

Betty, perched on a box, was reaching up for a peach. Her face was hot and dirty, but she smiled at Carl.

"I picked them all," she said, "so you can buy your bicycle right today." She smiled harder than ever. "Are you surprised?"

"Count to ten before you speak when you are angry," Dad always said.

Carl counted to thirty-seven before he could answer Betty.

"Yes," he said slowly, "I certainly am surprised." He could hardly get the words out. "Run in, and have your nap now."

Betty hurried off into the house.

"Why, oh, why," thought Carl, "did I ever tell her that she could help me pick the peaches? Why, oh, why did I tell her they had to be a lot bigger instead of telling her that they had to be red and yellow besides?"

Carl went off behind the barn and sat down, just in case he might cry. There wasn't any way to earn money for a bicycle now. And besides, Dad needed him to help with the peaches.

Maybe in the fall, though—but then a horrible thought came to him. Suppose Freddy sold the bicycle to somebody else!

Carl shrugged his shoulders and started for the house. He was very busy every day after that. He helped Dad with any job he could think of and played with Betty whenever his mother was busy.

Before Carl knew it, the big red-and-blue tent that Dad used for a fruit stand was set up in the front yard, with the baskets of peaches under it.

Carl always liked the peach season, and he did this year, too, except when he started thinking about how none of the nice yellow peaches were from his own tree. But mostly he was too busy to worry about that, because this year Dad let him run the stand.

One day a man stopped at the fruit stand. He didn't seem to be satisfied with anything Carl had.

"My name's Martin," he said. "I want the biggest, nicest peaches on the place. I'm going to send them by plane to my daughter up North and show her what kind of things they grow in this part of the world."

Carl showed the man all the different kinds of peaches he had. None of them were big enough.

"Why don't you sell him those on your own tree?" asked Carl's biggest brother, bringing a load of peaches in from the orchard.

"I don't have any on my tree," said Carl.

"Not many, maybe, but what there are—oh, boy!" exclaimed his brother.

"Lead me to them!" said Mr. Martin.

"Just step across the road," said Carl. He didn't really think anything was going to come of those peaches. Surely his brother had been looking at the wrong tree.

Carl walked under the tree, pushed his head up through the branches, and looked through the many leaves.

"Oh, my!" said Carl, with his mouth wide open in surprise.

There, deep in the dark green and far out of the reach of Betty's fingers were some of the biggest peaches Carl had ever seen.

"Big as footballs!" said Mr. Martin, sticking his head up through the branches, too. "Exactly what I want!"

They weren't really as big as footballs, but they were as big as Carl's softball. Carl couldn't imagine how they got so big until he remembered what Dad had said once.

"If a tree doesn't have many peaches on it," Dad said, "it turns all its strength into the few it has and you get something extra nice and extra big."

"How many of these do you have?" asked Mr. Martin, rubbing his hands together. "I'll take them all!"

"I don't know, sir," said Carl, pushing the leaves to one side and uncovering still more peaches at the top of the tree. "A half-bushel maybe, or maybe more."

"And first-class peaches, every one," said Mr. Martin. "I'll give you a first-class price. What would you say to five dollars for the lot?"

"I'd say fine," said Carl. "I'll pick them right now!"

"My daughter will be eating peaches tomorrow," said Mr. Martin excitedly. "My, won't she be surprised!"

"Not half so surprised as I am!" said Carl to himself.

Now Carl didn't have to squint up his eyes at all to see a big bicycle growing on his bicycle tree.

Mildred Lawrence

If I Were a Tree

If I were a little tree like you,
    Instead of a child like me,
I would dig my roots in the good black earth
    And toss my arms to the sea.
I would be twisted and small like you
    For the winds to bend me low,
And drops of rain on my twigs would lie
    Like silver beads in a row.
I would be like you as ever I could—
    Green-spiked and needle-y,
If I were a little tree like you,
    Instead of a child like me!

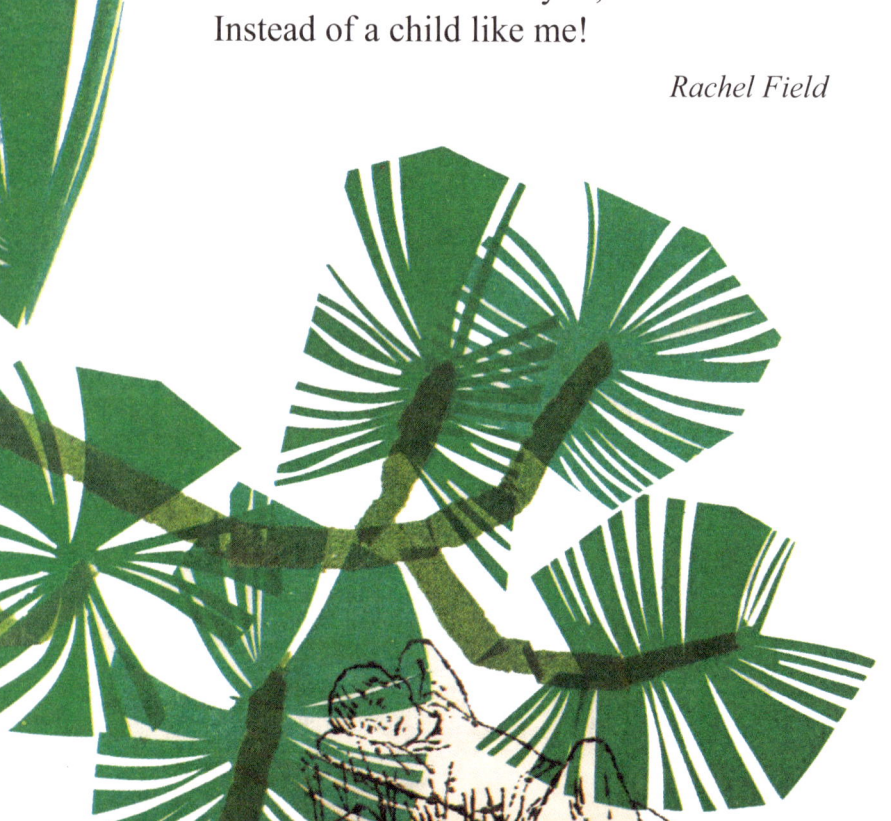

Rachel Field

The Chickens That Stayed Up

Joseph Lind was going for a visit. His friend David Carter had invited him to come and spend a week at the Carter Dairy Farm.

Mr. Carter and David came for Joseph in a large truck. They took him to their farm which was in another county about thirty-five miles away from Honey Spring Valley.

Joseph had a wonderful visit with his friend. He had a good time looking over the big dairy farm. He had never seen so many cows at once. There were seventy-five milking cows in all.

He was happy to have a chance to help David take care of his calf. It was a very important calf that David was raising all by himself. He had learned how to take care of the calf through the 4-H Club to which he belonged.

One day while the two boys were giving the calf a bath, David said, "I will take my calf to the county fair this fall. I hope he will look good and healthy enough to be a prize winner."

David's 4-H Club had a meeting while Joseph was there. Joseph went to it with his friend. Joseph was too young to be a member of the 4-H Club, but it was fun to be able to go to a meeting.

Joseph told the boys and girls all about Honey Spring Valley and the new 4-H Club. They liked "The Happy Honeys" for a club name.

There were eleven boys in David's 4-H Club. Most of them were raising calves or poultry.

Joseph liked chickens and was pleased to have a chance to hear the boys talking about raising them.

Then one evening while Joseph was still at the Carter Farm, Mr. Carter asked him if he would like to visit a large poultry farm. Joseph opened his eyes wide in surprise. It was almost dark, and he wondered what they could see at the poultry farm after dark.

"Won't it bother the chickens if we go this late in the evening?" Joseph asked Mr. Carter.

The Carter family laughed. "Just you wait and see," said David.

They went to the White Poultry Farm in Mr. Carter's truck. It was one of the largest poultry farms in the county, and Joseph saw many long, low, white houses.

"I hope we don't bother the hens," Joseph said again. He thought of the loud noises hens made when they were awakened from their sleep.

Mr. White led Joseph to one of the henhouses. Lights were shining in the windows. He opened the door.

What a busy place! Bright lights shone through the whole henhouse. It was as bright as day.

Busy hens were scratching and eating. Many of them were laying eggs. It was after dark, but the speckled hens were working as if the sun were shining.

Joseph was so very surprised that he hardly believed his own eyes. "What hard working chickens!" he exclaimed.

"That is exactly the reason the lights are on," laughed Mr. White. "It makes the chickens work longer. In this way more of them lay eggs each day. Then I have more eggs to sell."

Joseph was surprised to see that every single chicken had its own cage with its own food. The chickens' cages were in long rows. Every time one of the chickens laid an egg, it came rolling out in front of the cage. This made it easier for the farmer to gather the eggs.

Mr. White said to Joseph, "I will show you something even more interesting than this."

He took the two boys to another low house. It was the home of the baby chicks. In the middle of the floor was a low silver-looking box with a pointed roof on it. Many baby chicks that looked just alike were running in and out of the little doors.

"What sort of thing is that?" asked Joseph.

"That is an electric heater," answered Mr. White. "The heater keeps the little chickens warm."

Here, too, the electric lights were on. The henhouse was as bright as day. The baby chicks were busy eating. They scratched about all around the electric heater, making little chirping noises.

"My chickens grow very fast," Mr. White said.

"No wonder!" said Joseph, looking at the greedy chicks eating and eating.

Joseph enjoyed his visit very much. When he returned home at the end of the week, he had many interesting things to share with his friends. He liked to tell about helping to feed the seventy-five cows, but best of all he liked to tell about the chickens that stayed up at night.

Presents for Mother

What Will It Be?

"We've done a pretty good job if you ask me," said Michael Parks, sitting down on his bed. "Now if you two will move the empty trunks out, *my* room will be in good shape."

The Parks family had just moved to the big farmhouse from a city apartment, and the children were helping Mother to clean up and put things away.

"You just do some moving yourself, Mr. Bossy," said Michael's sister Barbara. "Andy's too little to help."

"I don't want to move the trunks anyway," Andy said, crawling under the bed as he spoke. "Come and play hiding with me."

Usually, nine-year-old Barbara was willing to play anything, but today she had a problem on her mind.

Mother's birthday will be here soon," she said.

"Oh, it's days and days until Mother's birthday," Andy said cheerfully from under the bed.

"Not so many days at that," said Michael. "Has anybody thought of a present for Mother yet?"

"Not I," Barbara answered. "I've been thinking about it for weeks. The beads I gave her last year went to a church fair. I remember that."

"I wish we could get together and give her something she would really want to keep," said Michael.

"She'd keep it, I think, if she remembered we gave it to her," said Barbara, "but she forgets so quickly."

"The real trouble is that we get her what we like ourselves. I'm certain, if we get her something that's important to her, she'll keep it."

Michael jumped off the bed. "Why, all we have to do," he cried, "is to ask her what she wants."

Barbara shook her head. "No good," she said. "I tried that. She said this old farmhouse was the best birthday present she could have. She has always wanted to live in the country."

"But it's not a surprise," said Michael, "and it belongs to all of us. And besides, we didn't give it to her."

"I know," Barbara agreed.

At that moment Andy popped his head out from under the bed. "I know what she wants," he said.

"How do you know?" asked Barbara.

Andy's round little face grinned up at her like an elf. "I heard her say so."

"When? What did she say?" Michael wanted to know.

"It was the day she and Daddy bought the house," Andy began. "She said there was a lot of land around, even room enough to keep chickens and have our own fresh eggs."

"That's right," Barbara exclaimed. "In the city she always wished the eggs were fresher."

"Come on," said Michael. "There's a sign up the road that says *Eggs for Sale*. Let's see if they'd sell us three chickens, one from each of us to give Mother."

The idea sounded wonderful to everyone.

In a very short time the three children arrived, breathless, at the nearby farmhouse door. It was opened by a large woman with gray hair and a round, cheerful face.

"Hello," she greeted them. "Come right in. You're the new city folks from down the road, I guess."

"Yes," Michael replied. "We came to ask about chickens. Do you sell them?"

"Indeed we do, if you don't want them in too much of a hurry," said the woman.

"Oh, we don't want them until a week from Saturday," said Michael. "We'd like three."

"I suppose you want them dressed," the woman said.

Andy laughed. Dressed?" he asked. "You don't *dress* them, do you?"

The farmer's wife laughed, too. "Not in clothes," she said. "I pluck them and clean them for roasting, if your mother can't do it."

"Oh, NO!" the children cried.

"We want them alive," Michael explained, "for a present, you know. We want to give Mother what she really wants for her birthday."

The woman was very much interested. She asked a number of questions, and before long Michael was counting out their money on the kitchen table.

Soon the whole matter was settled.

It was not until a week from Saturday afternoon that things really began to happen. At first it seemed as if there would never be a chance to bring the chickens home without Mother's seeing them. After all, there are few presents so hard to hide as full-grown chickens.

Finally, late in the afternoon, Mother remembered something she had to get at the store. She and Daddy set out in the car.

"Come on," Michael said. "There's not a minute to lose. We not only have to get those chickens home, we have to get them to sleep before Mother comes back."

The chickens were waiting for them in the farm kitchen: one white hen, one speckled hen, and a fine large rooster.

At once Michael picked up the rooster, and the three children started down the road, each with a chicken in his arms.

A Country Birthday

On the way Michael had a bright idea. "Let's name them for ourselves," he said. "Then Mother can't ever forget that we gave them to her."

His sister was delighted and at once spoke to the white hen she was carrying. "Hello, Barbara," she said.

But Andy stopped in the middle of the road. "I want to go back and change mine," he said.

"Why?" asked the others.

"Because it's a girl. You can't call a girl chicken Andy," he said.

"Wait a minute," said Barbara. "Why don't we call your hen Ann? Lots of girls are named for their fathers that way, and I'm sure a hen named Ann would always make Mother think of Andy."

Andy thought it was a good idea, so they started home again.

Soon the three children and the three chickens were in Michael's bedroom. They had chosen that hiding place because the room was at the far end of the house, where a few noises might not be heard.

"We must slip out quietly, one at a time, and leave the chickens in the dark," whispered Michael. "Then they'll be quiet."

Very early Sunday morning, while it was still dark outside, Mrs. Parks woke up. At first she lay with her eyes closed, thinking how nice it was to live in the country and hear the rooster crowing. Then she sat straight up in bed.

"Jim," she cried. "There's a rooster in the house!"

"Don't be silly," her husband said in a sleepy voice.

"Listen," cried Mrs. Parks.

A rooster crowed again. "Cock-a-doodle-doo." It was fairly close by, certainly under the same roof.

"Oh, well," Mr. Parks said, "the windows are open, and a rooster may have flown in. It can't do any harm. Leave it alone until morning."

"I don't like the idea of their flying in like that," his wife replied. "Does it often happen on farms? Oh, dear, it's wakened the children."

There were strange sounds in the hall outside—laughs, crowing, and scampering feet. And then, "Happy Birthday!" shouted three voices.

The bedroom door was pushed open, and the children came into the darkness. Andy reached his mother's bed first and dropped the speckled hen right on top of her.

Mrs. Parks screamed. She could not see the hen, and it gave her a very strange feeling as it landed in the middle of her and then hopped off again. "Help!" she cried. "What is it?"

At that moment Michael and Barbara presented their gifts. The bed seemed full of odd creatures.

"Oh, turn on the light," cried Mrs. Parks. "Turn on the light!"

In the darkness her husband found the lamp and suddenly turned it on.

"Chickens!" gasped Mrs. Parks.

The children wondered if she was pleased. They stood very still, feeling somewhat worried. Then suddenly both Father and Mother began to laugh. They laughed so hard that the children laughed too, although they weren't quite sure what the joke was.

"Aren't they beautiful chickens?" asked Andy. "You know you said you wanted them. We named them for ourselves so you'd have something to remember us by, only the speckled hen is Ann instead of Andy, because of being a girl."

That made Mrs. Parks laugh more than ever.

"You are happy, aren't you, Mother?" asked Barbara. "Michael is making a coop, and you know how you like fresh eggs. You won't give them away, will you?"

Mrs. Parks shook her head. "I certainly won't," she said. "I'll keep them until they are very, very old. What's more, I shall never, never forget their names."

Robin Palmer

The Bread of Life

Jack Hunt and his father had decided to grow wheat on their farm one season. One day when they were preparing a field for the first planting, Mr. Hunt said, "Son, have you ever stopped to think how very important a crop of wheat can be? We need it for a number of things."

"Yes, Dad," agreed Jack, and his mouth began to water. "Maybe some of the wheat that we grow right here on our farm will be used for loaves of bread, cakes, cookies, pancakes, sweet buns, and crackers."

"My son," said Mr. Hunt, "you have forgotten something far more important than all those things. Wheat is used also for the 'Bread of Life.'"

Jack thought for a moment. Then he said excitedly, "I know what you mean, Dad. Wheat is used to make the altar breads which are changed into the Body of Christ in every Holy Mass."

As Jack and his father worked, Jack recalled this story about Our Lord's first promise to give Himself to us in the Sacrament of Holy Communion.

It happened the very day after Jesus had fed over five thousand people with only two fishes and five loaves of bread.

When all the people had eaten and understood what Our Lord had done for them, they felt sure that He was the Savior promised to them by God. They decided to take Jesus by force and make Him their king.

Our Lord understood why they wanted to make Him their king. It was not because they believed Him to be the Savior, the Son of God. It was not because they really loved Him. It was only because He had worked a miracle to feed them.

They thought the Savior could do other wonderful things for them, too. He might give them riches and all the good things of this world.

Jesus called His apostles away from the crowd. He told them to get into their boat and cross over to the city on the other side of the sea. Then Jesus went up to the mountain to pray.

Now, many of the people were very disappointed because Jesus had refused to be made a king. They decided to camp out near the hillside, and they slept there until morning.

"Maybe He will change His mind by tomorrow," they told one another.

In the meantime, the apostles were having great trouble on the sea. For hours they had rowed, but the wind was so strong that they had gone only a small part of the way. They felt worried, afraid, and very tired.

While they were still on the waters the apostles saw something very strange. Jesus was walking on the water and coming toward them. At first the apostles were frightened.

Jesus called to them over the waves, "Do not be afraid. It is I."

When Jesus reached the boat and got into it, the sea became quiet. Soon the boat reached the other side.

The apostles were now more surprised than ever. They had seen two great miracles within only a few hours.

When people in the city heard that Jesus had come, they ran out of their homes to see Him. Even those who had camped out all night rowed across the water to be with Our Lord and to try again to make Him their king.

"Master, when did You come here? How did You get here?" they asked as they crowded around Him.

Our Lord looked at the people. His eyes were filled with sadness as He said, "You have come looking for Me not because you believe in Me, but only because I gave you food to eat."

Jesus then spoke to the people and told them that He had not come into this world to give us the things of this life. He would give us another kind of food which would give us life everlasting.

"Master, give us this food always," the people cried out.

The people soon became surprised and disappointed when they heard what Jesus was telling them.

"I am the Living Bread that has come down from heaven," said Jesus, "and if anyone eat this Bread, he shall live forever."

Never before had the people heard anything like this. They looked at each other and asked, "Isn't this Jesus, the Son of Joseph and Mary? How can He say that He came down from heaven?"

Now, Jesus knew what the people were thinking and saying.

Jesus meant every word that He had already spoken to them. Then He began to speak once again.

"Unless you eat the Flesh of the Son of Man and drink His Blood, you shall not have life in you. He who eats My Flesh and drinks My Blood has everlasting life, and I shall raise him up on the last day. For My Flesh is food indeed, and My Blood is drink indeed."

This was too much for the people. One by one they walked away from Our Lord. That day many of His best friends left Him and never again listened to His words.

When Jesus saw His followers go away, He looked at the apostles and asked, Will you also leave Me?"

At once Peter knelt down and, looking up into the face of Jesus, said, "Lord, to whom shall we go? You alone have the words of eternal life."

Valley Pets

Pets—both large and small—are raised by the children of Honey Spring Valley.

Familiar Friends

The horses, the pigs,
And the chickens,
The turkeys, the ducks,
And the sheep!
I can see all my friends
From my window
As soon as I waken
From sleep.

The cat on the fence
Is out walking.
The geese have gone down
For a swim.
The pony comes trotting
Right up to the gate;
He knows I have candy
For him.

The cows in the pasture
Are switching
Their tails to keep off
The flies.
And the old mother dog
Has come out in the yard
With five pups to give me
A surprise.

James S. Tippett

Good Old Kristie

Early one June morning Elmer and Erik woke up and ran out to get their horse. They wanted to drive Kristie to the lake, so they could go swimming.

Elmer, who was just a little taller than his twin Erik, ran into the barn to get Kristie's hat. It was not on the nail where it belonged. It was nowhere to be found.

"Now we can't go to the lake," said Elmer sadly.

"Kristie will never move without her hat," said Erik as a tear came to his eye.

Now, this may seem strange to you, but Kristie was a odd creature. She was like many other horses in some ways. She had a head on the end of her neck, though the neck was rather thin. She had a leg at each corner, though the legs were rather crooked and bones stuck out here and there.

Kristie was different from many horses, for she had some funny ways. One was that she would not move unless she had her hat on, and now her hat was gone.

"What can we do?" asked the twins. "What can we do?"

They both wanted to go swimming very much. The only way to get to the lake was to drive Kristie, for it was too far away to walk.

Elmer and Erik looked everywhere for Kristie's hat. They looked in the well house and in the cornhouse. Then they looked in the pig lot.

Kristie's hat was there, but the pigs were eating it up as fast as they could. Only a small piece of the hat stuck out of their mouths, but it was not enough to make Kristie move.

The twins' father came out to see what the trouble was. He saw the pigs eating Kristie's hat. There was only one straw of the old hat left by that time.

Father plucked off his own straw hat. He pulled out his knife, slipped it into his hat, and cut a long hole in each side. Elmer and Erik knew at once that it was for their horse's head.

The twins led Kristie from the barn and hitched her to the wagon. Their father put his hat on her head and pulled her ears through the holes. He tied it under her neck.

Kristie did not like the hat at all. It hurt her ears and tickled her neck because the brim was too wide.

All Kristie would do was to dance up and down on her crooked legs.

"Well, that will not do," said Father as he plucked his hat off Kristie's head.

Elmer and Erik ran into the house for their old hats. They cut large, long holes in each side for Kristie's ears. The holes were very large, but the hats were too small. They would not even go over Kristie's ears. All she would do was kick and shake from side to side.

"These hats will never make Kristie go," said Elmer and Erik as they tried to keep tears from their eyes.

By this time the twins' mother and the hired man were at the barn. They knew how much Elmer and Erik had wanted a horse when they first moved to Honey Spring Valley several months ago.

They knew that Elmer and Erik had saved all their spending money and all the money that they got from selling eggs and blackberries to pay for Kristie.

But what good was a horse that would not go?

"You can borrow my hat," said the hired man, "only don't bother cutting the holes until we see if Kristie likes it."

Father held Kristie's ears together and Elmer and Erik pulled the hat down over them. Kristie did not like that hat at all. She whinnied and tossed her head high, and the hat went flying through the air, with the hired man running after it.

"What can we do?" cried Elmer and Erik. "Kristie is so strange about her hats. She must have just the right hat, or she'll never go again."

The twins looked at their mother. Their father looked at her, too, and so did the hired man. Even Kristie seemed to be looking at her.

Father pulled his hat down on his own head. Some of his hair stuck out through the holes. "I suppose there is no other old hat in the house or in a trunk somewhere," he said.

"No old hat," said Mother, walking slowly, very slowly, toward the house.

Soon Mother came back carrying her hat. It was the black hat she wore to town on Saturday nights. It was made of good, soft straw and was a fine round shape. There was a red rose bobbing over the front brim.

"Kristie can have this if she wants it," Mother said. "I can borrow it from her if I really need it again."

Father cut holes in the hat, but this time he was careful not to make them too large in case Kristie didn't like the hat. Mother put two pieces of ribbon on the hat for ties.

Then Elmer and Erik put the hat on Kristie's head and carefully pulled her ears through the holes. Erik tied the ribbons in a bow under Kristie's chin.

Everyone stood very still waiting to see what Kristie would do. Kristie whinnied and nodded her head, and the red rose bobbed over the brim. Then Kristie started walking around just as a horse should do.

"She likes it," said Elmer, grinning.

"Oh, she does," said Erik, climbing in the wagon to which Kristie was hitched.

"Good old Kristie," everyone said.

Elmer and Erik had never been so happy. They had the thing that they wanted most in the world—a horse. They also had a horse that would move as any horse should.

Emma Brock

Joseph and His Banty

A storm was brewing. The sky was a strange color. The air seemed to be pushing down on the farm buildings, the crops, the animals, and the people.

Everything in the valley was calm and quiet. The cows were not mooing. The hens were not clucking. Even the leaves on the oak trees were very still.

It seemed to Joseph Lind that everything in the valley was only waiting—waiting for the storm to strike.

"Come, Sara, Joseph, and Tommy. Come inside now," called Mrs. Lind from the kitchen door.

As soon as the family was together they all knelt down with their rosary beads and prayed. While they were praying, the wind started to blow. At first it sounded rather low and gentle. Then in about thirty minutes it became louder and louder until it was fierce and frightening.

The Linds and everyone else in the valley had to eat by candlelight that night because the electric lights were off.

"I wish we had a new roof on our house," said Sara as they sat down to eat supper.

"A new roof wouldn't mean a thing in a windstorm like this," said Mr. Lind.

"Did you get all the chickens into the barn?" Mother asked.

Father nodded.

A strange feeling suddenly came over Joseph. "Did you get Banty in, too?" he asked his father.

"Banty is your pet hen, Joseph," said Mr. Lind. "I didn't have a minute to lose in taking care of the laying hens."

"Mother went after the horse, and I helped to get the cow into the barn," boasted Tommy.

"Why didn't you take care of Banty yourself?" asked Sara.

"I did, sort of," Joseph answered slowly. "I put her into the new coop."

"Ho-ho!" laughed Sara. "That little coop you made isn't going to stay on the ground two minutes in a storm like this."

Joseph gasped. The wind was getting stronger all the time. He remembered that once before in a bad storm a neighbor's barn was picked up and carried down the road by the wind.

"I'm sorry, Joseph," said his father, "but we had all we could do to take care of the useful animals."

"Banty can't give milk or even lay an egg," Tommy said with laughter.

"It's time to go to bed," Mother said. "We'll just hope that Banty is safe."

Before long the family was sleeping—all but Joseph. He tried with all his strength not to think of Banty, but it was no use. He should have taken better care of his hen. He thought unhappily of losing her. He thought of his pet being carried miles away by the force of the strong wind.

Even though he was tired, Joseph was unable to sleep.

Suddenly, the wind died down.

Joseph thought the storm was over, and so he got up, took a flashlight, and slipped out into the night.

Outdoors everything was quiet and black. Joseph flashed the light toward the barn. It was still standing, but the empty henhouse was turned over on its side. He looked for Banty's little coop. It was gone.

"Here, Banty! Here, Banty!" Joseph called. There was no answer.

He walked around and called again, but still there was no answer. Joseph shone the light up at the house. It was unharmed.

All at once Joseph heard a tiny cluck-cluck coming from the oak tree. He flashed the light up toward the tree. Sure enough, there was Banty's coop perched in the tree where the wind had blown it.

Joseph quickly put the flashlight into his jacket pocket and began climbing up the tree. It was a tree he had often climbed, and soon he was beside the coop.

Banty was still in the coop, but was unharmed. Joseph quickly placed her inside of his jacket and zipped it up. As he started to climb down, the tree suddenly gave a terrible jerk. The storm was returning.

With all his strength Joseph held fast to the branches to keep from falling. The flashlight dropped from his pocket and was lost somewhere in the darkness below. Slowly Joseph made his way to the ground, holding his pet close to him.

He tried to crawl toward the house, but the wind forced him back against the tree. The noise of the wind was all Joseph could hear. It seemed to him that there was nothing anywhere except the horrible screaming wind, twisting and doing whatever it wanted with everything in its way.

Joseph had to get back to the house someway, but the wind kept pushing him and driving small things at him, like arrows shooting from bows. Sharp rocks, pieces of wood, and hay cut him.

Fearfully he called out for help, but no one heard him because the wind was so noisy.

While Joseph was trying to decide what to do, the wind suddenly changed. Lifting him from the ground, it twisted him wildly. Then he found himself falling. He landed hard on the back steps—sore, dirty, and breathless.

He found the door and banged on it. The door opened, and his father pulled him inside quickly.

Joseph fell on the floor, and out of his jacket crawled Banty.

"Joseph!" exclaimed his mother. Then she leaned down to put cold wet cloths on his head and his pale scratched face.

After a few minutes Joseph opened his eyes. He was in his own bed, and he saw his family around him.

"I thought the storm was over," he said. "I went to find Banty." A worried look came over his face as he asked breathlessly, "Where is she?"

"She's right here," said his mother, "on the foot of your bed."

Joseph smiled and was soon sleeping.

The next morning, when the storm was over, Joseph was awakened by Banty's proud clucking. On the foot of Joseph's bed was a little brown egg—the first one Banty had ever laid.

"It's just the right size for Joseph's breakfast," said his mother.

"Banty laid that egg for Joseph," said Tommy. "She is thanking him for bringing her in from the storm."

Marguerite Gallien

Wanted: Two Kids

"Two kids for sale," said the radio announcer for the Farmer's Market Program. "You can get them by going to Apple Orchard Farm. To get there, go on County Road 133. Turn left at the first crossroad, right at the next, and stop at the first farm on the left."

Peter and Peggy Winters ran excitedly to their mother. "Kids are baby goats, aren't they, Mother?" Peter cried. "You told us that we could use our birthday money to buy our own pets. Would two goats be all right?"

261

Mother smiled down at the children's eager faces. "I don't know why little goats wouldn't be all right," she replied. "We have plenty of rough pasture for them. We'll have to settle the matter with your father first of all."

"I'll get some paper and write down the directions to Apple Orchard Farm," said Peggy. "The announcer said to go out County Road 133, didn't he?"

Peter nodded and then said the exact words that the radio announcer had used. He was proud of the way that he could always remember things.

When Mr. Winters heard the news, he was as pleased as the children. "I had a pet goat when I was a boy, and it was a fine playmate," he told them.

He decided to take the children to Apple Orchard Farm that very evening.

"Let's get in the car now and go to find the goats before dark," he said.

"Don't forget to bring the directions along," Father called to Peggy.

When the family got to County Road 133, Mr. Winters stopped the car and asked, "Now which way do we turn—to the north or south?"

Peggy gave the directions to him. "Let's see," he said. "The directions say to take County Road 133, but they don't say which way to go on 133."

Peter and Peggy suddenly looked quite disappointed.

"Could we try both ways?" Peter asked.

"Of course we can," answered Mother. "Our supper can wait."

"Don't worry," said Mr. Winters to the children. "We'll find the place."

But they didn't. They turned north and rode down the road and then back again. They rode toward the south on County Road 133, but they couldn't find Apple Orchard Farm.

It was dark by the time they were back in front of their own house again without the goats.

"I know what we can do," said Peggy as the family sat down to their late supper. "We can call the radio station and ask the announcer for the goat owner's name and telephone number. Then we can call the owner and find out exactly how to get to his farm."

"That's a good idea, Peggy," said Mr. Winters. "We'll call the station right after supper."

The people at the radio station could not find the letter from the person who owned the kids. They said they would announce that someone wanted to buy two baby goats. Then perhaps the owner would hear it and answer.

The telephone rang twice the next morning, and both Peter and Peggy ran to answer it.

The first time the phone rang, it was a call from a lady who wanted Mrs. Winters to serve on a citizens' committee. The second call was about a secondhand trailer that Mr. Winters wanted to sell or trade. The next few days were just as disappointing.

Finally, Peter thought of another idea. "Many people go into town on Saturday," he said. "If we make a large sign saying that we want to buy two baby goats, someone will see it and tell us where to get them."

Early that evening, with their parents' help, Peter and Peggy made a large sign with black ink.

> Wanted: Two Young Goats

The next morning soon after they woke up, Peter and Peggy placed the sign on the fence in front of their house and waited.

Quite a few drivers slowed to read the sign, but not a single one stopped. Peggy and Peter were becoming more and more disappointed.

Shortly after eleven o'clock, an old pick-up truck stopped in front of the Winters' house. A fat little woman looked out, squinted her eyes, and read the sign. Then she turned into the driveway and called out to Peggy and Peter.

"You want to buy two kids?" she asked. "I've got two in the back of the truck."

Both children hurried to the truck as the woman got out.

"There they are," said the fat little woman, waving her arm toward two kids that looked just alike. "I had it announced on the radio that they were for sale, but no one seemed interested. So I decided to take them to the sale at the County Fair."

"Oh, we were interested," explained Peggy, staring longingly at the friendly little animals, "but our problem was that we couldn't find your farm."

The fat little woman threw her head back and laughed so hard that her whole body shook. "I guess I always make mistakes in giving directions. My son always did say that I get things mixed up, but all's well that ends well. I think we can settle on a price. Do you want these little fellows?"

"We sure do," exclaimed Peggy and Peter, grinning and climbing into the truck to make friends with their new playmates.

The children had already decided on names for their new pets. Peter named his kid North, and Peggy named hers South. Perhaps you can guess why they chose such strange names.

Dorothy Patterson Gault

Pepper the Pony

One summer Billy Butterfield was visiting his uncle on a ranch out West. Billy was used to farm animals, but getting used to a ranch horse was something new for him.

As Billy limped down a crooked path toward his uncle's house, he looked down into the valley at the empty, flat pasture. Rocket, his uncle's horse, was not there.

"That means that Uncle Frank has not returned from town," he thought.

Billy limped on, his foot hurting badly, for it was a long walk from the church where he had gone.

It had been only a week since he had told his uncle how much he would like to have a cow pony of his own. Now the very thought of it made him fearful.

How could he ever have thought he wanted a horse? Today he wanted nothing at all to do with the creatures. He had had enough. Never again would he say one word about a cow pony, and he hoped his uncle would forget about it.

Billy sighed and limped on toward the house. There Aunt Dorothy was making doughnuts and several loaves of bread. When she saw Billy, she said, "Hello! How's the sore foot?"

"It's pretty sore yet," Billy answered quietly.

"Your uncle never should have allowed you to ride that horse of his," said Billy's aunt. "Rocket is so wild."

Billy well remembered how he had flown through the air when his uncle's horse had tossed him off the day before.

"Help yourself to some doughnuts," Aunt Dorothy said to Billy. "Then, when you're finished eating doughnuts, you had better feed the chickens. I don't know when Uncle Frank will be home."

After Billy had finished his chores, he heard the clatter of hoofs and a horse whinny. Then he saw his uncle riding Rocket toward the ranch. There was a small pony trotting along beside him.

For a moment Billy felt frozen to the ground. "Could that pony be for me?" he wondered.

Quickly he went into the house and ran to his room. He took out a book, turned on the lamp, and tried to read. Maybe his uncle wouldn't ask him to go outside if he seemed interested in the book.

At supper that evening nothing was said about Rocket or about the pony.

The next morning, almost before Billy had finished eating his eggs and oatmeal, his uncle called, "Billy! Come and see what is out here!"

Billy felt very uneasy as he called, "Coming, Uncle Frank."

There at the back door stood the cow pony he had seen the day before.

"Like her, Billy?" asked his uncle. She's yours! Her name is Pepper."

"She's a beauty!" Billy said, but he really didn't mean it.

"Well, she's ready to go. Let's see you ride her," exclaimed his uncle.

As Billy climbed up, feeling weak and fearful, the pony jerked and pawed the ground. "That's a sure sign she doesn't like me," Billy thought to himself.

Then Uncle Frank cried, "Gid-ap, Pepper, gid-ap!" Off sailed the pony in a wild gallop, throwing a spray of dust up as her hoofs touched the dry dirt.

"Oh, if only I can hang on until the pony is tired and wants to stop!" Billy gasped.

After a while the pony slowed down to a trot.

"Whoa, girl! Whoa!" cried Billy, and Pepper obeyed and came to a quick stop. Billy was surprised that Pepper had obeyed him so well.

"Why, she likes me," he said out loud. "She would never throw me off her back. She's a wonderful little pony!"

All at once Billy's fear of horses was gone as quickly as it had come.

He jumped down and looked right into Pepper's face. "Good girl!" he said as he touched and then kissed her soft nose.

He climbed back on the pony. This time Pepper did not jerk or paw but stood very still. Billy was happy and was ready to gallop off when Uncle Frank came along on Rocket.

"Well, I didn't need to worry about you," Uncle Frank said. "For a little while, I was afraid that you would let Pepper run away with you. That's why I followed you."

"Pepper and I are going to get along very well together, thank you," replied Billy with a smile on his face.

"I knew all along how afraid and fearful you were after Rocket tossed you off his back," said Uncle Frank. "That's why I got the pony for you right away."

Billy grinned. "At first I thought maybe it would be better to keep away from horses until I wasn't afraid any more," he said.

"If you had done that, you would have waited a long, long time," said Billy's uncle. "It is strange, but the longer you wait, the more fearful you become. And you, my boy, have really lost your fears."

"Gid-ap, girl!" Billy cried. Pepper obeyed again and galloped off down the road.

Marjorie Pearson

Friends from a Valley Far Away

Carlos moved to Honey Spring Valley from a country called Mexico. For hours he would sit under his big hat, which he called a sombrero, telling stories about his friends in Mexico.

Beto's Many Sombreros

For many months Carlos' friend Beto had wanted a new sombrero. Every day he thought about what it would be like. For one thing, it would be black with many bright colors on it. It would have a wide brim with little colored balls hanging down along the edge.

When Beto told his mother about his wish, she said, "You already have many sombreros, little Beto. Why would you want another?" Even as she said this she turned her head and smiled. She already knew why.

"The new one would be for the great feast day," replied Beto. "For the first time in my life, I will be going to the festival with you and Papa."

Papa was listening as he ate his breakfast. "Little boys must earn new sombreros," he said.

"How can I do that?" asked Beto.

"In a family, when a boy does his work well, perhaps he can earn his wish. Who knows?" said Papa, shrugging his shoulders. "Now it is time for a boy called Beto to feed the turkeys and chickens and to gather the eggs."

Beto sighed as he walked over to the wall where his sombreros were hanging. He took an old straw one from the wall and put it on his head. It was dirty and torn at the edges. When Beto leaned over to feed the chickens, one of them reached for a straw in his old sombrero, thinking it was a piece of hay.

Beto found so many eggs that he had to carry them in his sombrero to the house, making three trips.

"This sombrero is good for carrying eggs, but it will never do to wear to the festival," Beto told his mother. "It's too old and torn."

"That is so," replied his mother, "but perhaps even a very old sombrero may help a boy to get his wish. Who knows?"

Soon it was time for Beto to get out the little gray burro and to go off to the market with the eggs.

"My small sombrero with the wide red band is the one I shall wear to the market," said Beto as he hung the old straw one back on the wall.

Papa helped Beto load the eggs in the baskets that hung on the little burro's sides. Then Beto jumped on the burro's back.

"Get a good price for the eggs, and remember to buy all the things Mama told you to get," said Papa. "Don't be slow about getting back for lunch."

After Beto sold all of his eggs, he bought the colorful beads and the buttons that Mama wanted. He wanted very much to visit the place where sombreros were sold, but it was getting late so he rode back home, wearing his small sombrero with the wide red band on it.

"This is a fine sombrero for going to market," he told his mother when he got home, "but it is too small to wear to the festival."

"That is so," his mother agreed, "but perhaps even a very small sombrero may help a young boy to get his wish. Who knows?"

After Beto had eaten his lunch, Mama said, "It is too warm to work. It is time now to take a nap."

Beto put on his biggest sombrero and started out to take a nap under a tree.

"This is a fine sombrero to wear for a nap," he told his mother. "It is big and keeps the sun off my face, but it is too big to wear to the festival. It would bump into all the dancers."

After supper that evening, Papa said to Beto, "Your mother and I are going to take some eggs to our neighbors. You must stay here in case the coyotes come to rob us of our turkeys and chickens."

Beto sat down by the door, watching his parents go down the road with a basket of eggs. Everything was quiet. The sun was just going down in the sky. The chickens and turkeys had flown up into the trees for the night.

Things were not quiet for very long. Soon the screaming and crying of a band of coyotes rang through the clear air. The sound came closer and closer. The chickens and turkeys moved around uneasily.

"What shall I do?" Beto thought. As he picked up a big stick, a thought suddenly came to him. He ran into the house and got all of his sombreros from the wall where they hung.

He turned on the lamp and put one of his sombreros in each of the windows. He put the tallest one on his head and began to march beside the house like a soldier with the stick over his shoulder.

Then louder and louder screamed the coyotes. Nearer and nearer they came. Faster and faster beat Beto's heart.

"What if the coyotes carry off our turkeys and chickens?" Beto thought. "Then there will be no eggs to sell and I will not earn a new sombrero."

Suddenly everything became very quiet. Beto could see the coyotes standing still and looking toward the house.

"I think I have tricked them," he said to himself. "They think there is a person under each sombrero and that I am a tall man with a gun."

Sure enough, the coyotes suddenly turned and ran in the other direction as fast as they could.

Just then Beto's mama and papa came home. "Oh, Beto! Beto!" they called. "Did the coyotes take our chickens and turkeys? We heard them screaming, but we could not get here any faster."

Papa and Mama smiled when they heard what Beto had done. "My sombreros helped me to gather the eggs, to go to the market, and to take a nap," the boy said. "Now they have helped me in another way. All the coyotes ran because they saw so many sombreros."

"Now you need one more sombrero—one that will help you dance at the festival," said Papa.

"We will sell some eggs and one or two of the chickens and turkeys that you saved from the coyotes. Perhaps there will be enough money to buy the very sombrero you want. Who knows?"

Mama smiled at Beto and said, "Your many sombreros have helped you find a way to get your wish."

The next week Beto danced at the festival wearing a new black sombrero with many bright colors on it and many little colored balls that hung down around the edges.

Betsy Warren

The Painted Cart
Terrible News

When Carlos lived in Mexico, he had a good friend named Pedro.

One day something terrible happened to a cart that Pedro's father had painted for the fair. Pedro had run all the way from his home to tell Carlos about it.

"The cart was full of straw," said Pedro, trying hard to fight back his tears. "I guess we had it too close to the fire. Before we knew it, the whole thing was burning."

Carlos dropped the basket of ripe beans he had in his hand. "Not the pretty little cart your papa painted just last week!" he cried.

Pedro nodded his head sadly. "Papa was trying to make it the prettiest cart in the town."

"What will you do?" asked Carlos. "Tomorrow is fair day. You will not be able to be in the parade, and I've heard that the prize for the prettiest cart this year is a calf."

"If only we could have won it," sighed Pedro. Then he shrugged his shoulders and added, "I guess we can ride to the fair in the cart, but we can't go in the parade because the paint is all burned off. Even the wheels are burned, and the cart looks brown and ugly."

Pedro sounded as if he didn't really care if he went to the fair.

Carlos stood still for a while after his friend had left him. From the place where he was working he could see the cart which his own father had painted for the fair parade. Papa had promised that if it was judged the prettiest, Carlos could have the prize.

"A calf of my very own!" he said to himself. Just thinking about it made Carlos feel happy all over. Now that Pedro's beautiful cart was burned, the one his father had painted would surely win the first prize.

Suddenly a terrible thought rushed through Carlos' head. Suppose something happened to his father's cart!

Carlos began to feel fearful. Now he understood how Pedro felt, and he wanted to help him.

He walked over to the field where his father was working and told him about Pedro's burned cart.

"What a shame!" exclaimed Papa. "Pedro's family always had one of the prettiest carts in the fair parade. What a shame!"

"Maybe if Pedro's papa had someone to help him, he could repaint the cart before tomorrow," said Carlos eagerly.

"Then he shall have help!" said his father suddenly. "Come, son!"

Down the road the two hurried until they came to a small white house.

"Good morning," said Carlos' father to the man who came out to meet them. It was Donno, one of their neighbors. Carlos told him all about Pedro's beautiful cart that had been burned.

Donno put on his big sombrero and said, "Yes, Pedro and his papa must have their cart painted for the parade. I will be glad to go along and help."

The three hurried on down the road until they came to Pedro's house.

Helpful Neighbors

Pedro stared at Carlos and the two men when he saw them coming.

"Don't worry about your cart," Carlos told him. "We are going to help your papa paint the cart all over again. It will be finished in time for the parade."

Pedro's face changed from frowns to smiles. "Come, Carlos," he said, "we will get the paint ready."

Soon everyone was busy. The two boys started painting the wheels.

By the middle of the afternoon the cart was finished. Each man had painted the pictures he could make best. There were pictures of bright colored flowers, animals, and birds. Each of the large wooden wheels was painted a different color.

"Perhaps you will still win the first prize," Carlos told his friend, but the very sound of the words made his heart sad. He wanted so much to win the calf.

The next morning by the time the sun began to rise in the east, everyone was up and busy. Carlos washed his sunburned face and fixed his black hair. Then he put on his very best clothes and his new shoes and stockings.

Just before he and his parents left home, they put a string of pretty flowers around the neck of their little burro. Then they hitched him to the cart and started off for the fair.

On the way Carlos and his family met Pedro and his mama and papa in their newly painted cart. They all laughed and sang as they rode along.

In the streets there were orchestras and bands playing music of all kinds. The slow clatter of burro hoofs mixed with the music, but all Carlos could think of was the prize calf.

Finally it was time for the cart parade. Carlos' father was first to drive his painted cart past the judges. Carlos saw them nodding and talking. He hoped with all his heart that the calf would soon be his.

When Pedro's father went by with his cart, the judges looked more pleased with its beauty.

After all the carts had passed by, the calf was led straight to Pedro's father. His cart had won.

"Oh, I didn't do the painting myself," Pedro's father told the judges.

"It was Carlos' idea to help us," said Pedro.

"Yes, the calf should go to Carlos," Pedro's father explained to the judges.

"I didn't do much of the painting," said Carlos. "I can't paint well enough."

Slowly the judges looked at each other. "Didn't anyone win the first prize?" they asked.

Finally, Pedro's father explained that his cart had been burned and that Carlos had gotten his father and Donno to help repaint it.

The judges spoke together for a little while. They took the calf away, and soon they came back with two little spotted pigs. One was given to Pedro and the other to Carlos.

Pedro's pig looked at him and said, "Oink! Oink!"

"Oink! Oink!" answered the other pig.

"I'm glad we each have a prize," said Carlos. "I believe that I shall like this little pig just as much as a calf."

Verna Turpin Borsky

The Thank-You Animals

In the valley in Mexico lived one of Carlos' playmates. The boy's name was Juan, and his sister's name was Maria.

One bright June day Juan and Maria sat under a tree near their small house looking at the beautiful new sandals their mother had made for them. Juan's were red, and Maria's were green.

The children were wondering what they could do to show their mother how very much they liked the new sandals—the first they had ever had. For some time they sat under the tree and thought and thought and thought.

Finally Juan said, "I know what we can do." He whispered something into Maria's ear so their mother could not hear it.

"That will be a fine surprise," said Maria. "Let's start right away."

The children ran into the house where their mother was baking corn cakes.

"Oh, may I please have a little cake, Mama?" Juan asked.

"To be sure, you may," answered his mother, and she handed him one of her freshly made cakes.

"May I please have one, too, Mama?" Maria asked.

"Indeed, yes," smiled Mother, and she gave Maria a corn cake.

The children thanked their mother and walked to another part of the room. "We will not be hungry now while we are gone," Juan whispered quietly to his sister.

They looked into a big box. "I will carry half," Juan whispered again to his sister, "and you carry the other half. Be sure to hide them so Mama won't see them."

The children took the things from the box and walked very quietly out of the house.

When they got outside, Juan called, "Pepe, come here."

A little gray burro came trotting around the corner of the house. He spread his front legs apart so he could stop. He spread his back legs apart so he could stop. His ears stood up straight, and his eyes looked as if he wanted to ask a question.

"We're going somewhere, Pepe," said Juan to the burro, "and you are going to take us."

The little burro stood still, and the two children climbed up on his back. Juan took hold of the rope that was around Pepe's neck. Maria took hold of her brother. Then Juan kicked the burro's sides with his new sandals to let him know they were ready to go.

Pretty soon Juan and Maria were down in the green valley where there was a market place.

"We will spread out our things on the ground and call out," said Juan. "Then people will see us."

"That's a good idea," replied Maria. "You call first."

Then Juan began calling, "Burros for sale! Burros for sale!"

Pepe pawed the ground and looked a little frightened just as if he knew what Juan was saying. Juan laughed and said, "I do not mean you, little pet."

Then Maria called, "Pigs for sale! Pigs for sale!"

Many people were walking around the market place buying the ripe fruits and vegetables, but no one even stopped to see the little burros and pigs.

Juan seemed worried. "I think no one will buy from us because we are so small," he told his sister.

"Oh, our pigs and burros are fine. I'm sure someone will buy them," said Maria.

In a few minutes an American girl stopped to look at the toy animals. Juan showed her five little burros standing in a row, and then he described how they were made.

"I made these out of clay, and I baked them in an oven in our backyard," he said. "I painted them gray so they would look like our own burro named Pepe."

Maria showed the girl five toy pigs standing in a row. "I made these out of clay, and I baked them in an oven in our backyard," she explained. "I painted them red and yellow and blue because toy pigs are always painted bright colors in Mexico."

The little American girl nodded her head and said, "They are just what I want to take back to my friends in my country. I will buy all of your toy animals."

Maria held out her little hand, and the American girl put three pieces of American money in it.

Juan held out his hand, and the American girl put three pieces of money in it.

Then the little girl picked up all the toy animals and carefully put them into a bag. "Good-bye," she called to Juan and Maria as she left them.

Juan and his sister walked around the market place until they found something they wanted to buy with their money. They handed the money to a man, and he gave them a package in return.

Then the two children ran back to get their burro, and they rode home on his back.

When they got near the house, they could see their mother at the door waiting for them. "Where have you been?" she asked.

"We've been to the market place and have sold all the little clay animals we made," Juan answered.

"We bought you something, Mama," said Maria in an excited manner. "We bought it with the money we got for our toy animals."

Juan took one end of the present and Maria took the other end of it. Then they handed the present to their mother.

"Oh, a scarf! A beautiful, new scarf!" cried Mother as she kissed her two children, but tears were in her eyes.

"You can wear it to church," said Juan. "Your old scarf is torn and almost worn out."

"Oh, it is a shame that you will not have your little toy animals to play with," said Mother.

"I have pretty red sandals instead," laughed Juan.

"I have green sandals," said Maria.

Now Mother's tears were gone and she was laughing. Juan and Maria were laughing, too. Pepe, the burro, just pointed his ears up straight to show that he too was happy.

Anabel Armour

Our Lady and the Indian
On a Mountainside in Mexico

One morning when Carlos went to Confirmation class at Holy Cross Church, Father Dale gave him a special holy picture. It showed our Blessed Mother dressed in colorful clothes and an Indian kneeling in front of her.

The other children wanted to know about the picture, and so Father Dale told them this true story that happened in Mexico many years ago.

One cold winter morning a poor Indian awakened before sunrise and left his little village. He started off for Mexico City, which was miles away.

The old Indian's name was Juan, which means John. He was a very good Catholic, and he loved the Blessed Virgin in a special way.

On this morning Juan wanted to hear Mass in honor of the Mother of God. Since there was no church in his own village, he decided to walk all the way to Mexico City.

As the old man walked along, a large, white cloud seemed to be floating down the mountainside toward him. Juan stood still and looked at the sight. He heard a sweet voice calling his name.

Juan hurried up the mountain. When he climbed nearer the strange sight, a bright light shone through the cloud.

Then something wonderful happened.

A very beautiful Lady appeared in the cloud. "Juan, come closer," she said.

When Juan stepped closer, the lovely Lady said, "I am the Mother of God. I want you to go to the bishop of Mexico and tell him to build a church in this place in my honor."

Kneeling before the beautiful Lady, Juan watched her disappear. Then he hurried on toward the city to do as she had asked. When he reached Mexico City, he went straight to the bishop's house and described what had happened.

Of course, the bishop found it hard to believe Juan, for he thought the poor Indian only imagined that he had seen the Blessed Virgin.

The bishop told Juan that if our Blessed Mother really wanted a church built, she herself would have to give a sign from heaven.

The poor Indian started home feeling very sad. When he walked down the mountain, the Blessed Virgin appeared again in gleaming robes.

Juan was happy to see the lovely Lady again, but he felt ashamed to tell her what the bishop had said.

"No one will listen to me," Juan said. "I am only a poor Indian. The bishop thinks I only imagined that I saw you."

Our Blessed Mother smiled at him. "Do not worry," she said. "Tell the bishop again that God wants a church built here in my honor."

You can imagine how afraid Juan was to return to the bishop, but he did exactly as Our Lady had told him.

Again the bishop only smiled and said, "We should like to build a church in Mary's honor, but how can we know that what you claim is true unless we are given a sign from heaven?"

The Indian left when he heard these words. As he walked slowly down the mountain, two of the bishop's servants followed him. The bishop had sent them to watch Juan and to see if the Blessed Virgin really appeared to him.

For a long while the servants followed Juan. Then suddenly he disappeared right before their eyes.

In the meantime the Blessed Virgin appeared again to the Indian. "Do not worry," she told him. "Come here again tomorrow, and you shall have the sign the bishop wishes."

The Sign

When Juan reached home that night, he found his uncle very ill. He was afraid to leave the sick man and stayed, kneeling at his bedside all through the night and all the next day.

Very early the following morning, just at daybreak, Juan thought his uncle was going to die. He decided to run to the city and get the priest. Then he remembered that he had not done as the Blessed Virgin had told him.

He started up the mountain worrying about it when suddenly Our Lady appeared again.

Juan fell at her feet, bowed his head, and told her about his sick uncle.

"Do not fear," said the holy Mother of God. "At this very moment your uncle is well again. You will not have to hurry for a priest."

Then our Blessed Lady said something which surprised Juan. "I want you to go to the top of this mountain and pick the roses you will find there," she said. "Put them into your cloak, and return here to me."

Now, never before had anyone seen roses blooming up on this mountain during the cold season.

"How could roses bloom in winter?" the Indian wondered, but he obeyed anyway and went to look for the roses.

Juan had a pleasant surprise when he reached the top of the mountain. There he found the most beautifully shaped roses in full bloom.

Very quickly he picked the roses, put them into his cloak, and hurried back to the Virgin. Our Blessed Lady put her lovely hands over the roses as if she were blessing them.

"Go now," she said. "Take these to the bishop. Tell him it is the sign for which he asked. Do not open your cloak until you see the bishop."

Now, the poor Indian was happy as he hurried to the bishop's palace. When he got there, the servants wondered why Juan had his cloak wrapped around him.

"What are you trying to hide in your cloak?" they asked.

Juan remembered what Mary had told him. He wrapped the cloak more tightly around himself to hide the roses.

When the bishop finally came in, Juan exclaimed happily, "Here is the sign you asked for. Our Blessed Mother has told me to bring it to you."

As Juan unwrapped his cloak the beautiful roses dropped to the floor.

The bishop was surprised and also a bit frightened when he saw the beautiful roses. He had a still greater surprise when he looked up and saw another wonderful sight. There on Juan's poor cloak was a most beautiful picture of the Blessed Virgin.

The bishop called all his servants into the room. They all knelt down and gave glory to God and His holy Mother.

The picture of Our Lady on Juan's cloak was hung in the largest church in Mexico City until the people built a new church in Mary's honor.

The church that the Blessed Virgin asked to have built is still standing near Mexico City. People from all over Mexico go there on Mary's special feast day.

The King's Highway

I saw her walking through the field,
   God's Mother with her Son,
And every little flower bell pealed
   To praise the Holy One.

Oh, every little rose upturned
   To wave as He did pass,
And every little sunbeam burned
   Its incense on the grass!

Oh, every little piping bird
   Did trumpet from the tree,
And every little lambkin heard,
   And danced, God's Lamb to see!

Rt. Rev. Hugh F. Blunt, LL.D.

To the Teacher

This Is Our Valley, Revised Edition, is the Advanced Third Reader of the Faith and Freedom Basic Readers and is to be used after the completion of *This Is Our Town*, Revised Edition. It is designed to provide growth in the basic reading skills for children in the second half of the third grade. This text introduces 417 new words, 383 of which (starred in the list below) can be recognized independently by the pupil through the application of various word-attack skills developed in the manuals of the preceding books of the series and reviewed in the manual accompanying this text.

The first phase of training in Christian social virtue culminates in this book with the theme centered on Christian solidarity. The story content of the book leads the reader to understand how men, bound together in a spiritual sense through membership in the Mystical Body of Christ, live, work, struggle, and share their joys in social harmony.

WORD LIST
UNIT I

7. folks	20. ...	33. smells*
	21. honey*	ham*
8. Andrew*	stick*	delicious
Larry*	hundreds*	34. mistake*
joking*	22. swarm*	35. enjoy*
9. sold*	smooth*	
dairy*	bark*	36. disappointed*
10. mouse*	23. good-sized*	sighed*
11. invited*	hive*	37. sir*
foolish*	24. smoke*	eagerly*
12. mice*	25. plenty*	pasture*
13. wink*	fresh*	38. rough*
14. ...		magazine*
15. ...	26. Quacken	since*
	bush*	39. ...
16. (Poem)	27. famous	40. chores*
	county*	pole*
17. pirate's*	inspector*	41. gun*
shore*	28. potatoes*	against*
creek*	dropped*	law*
18. fierce	29. unusual	42. stream*
spades*	30. Hans*	43. cheerful*
19. dig*	whole*	
decided*	31. ...	44. wander
	32. ...	reason*

45. vegetable*
    Jack*
46. quarrel*
    apart*
47. lonely*
    trailer*
    gas*
48. ...
49. tools*
50. motor*
    chapel*
51. miles*
    twice*
52. ...

UNIT II

53. ...

54. orphans*
    pioneer*
    cabins*
55. clear*
    sparkling*
    froze*
56. barrels
57. ...
58. snow*
    covered
59. knock*
60. begged*
    thin*
61. ...
62. chest*
    hung*
63. bucket*
    matter*
64. fruit*
65. disappeared*

66. Feather*
    weak*
67. threw*
    shoulder*
68. fawns*
    sniffed*
69. tightly*

70. drank*
71. shoot*

72. Tekakwitha
73. although
74. treated*
    sorrows*
75. several*
76. suffered*
77. prepared*
    soul*

78. present*
    bargain*
79. grandma*
    kettle*
    handle*
80. wolves
81. rather*
    delight*
82. ...
83. July*
    match*
    tonight*
84. ...
85. heavy*
86. lifted*
    spilled*
    chin*
87. ...
88. stockings*

89. January*
90. imagine*
    built*
91. sweaters*
    boiling*
92. gray*
93. ...
94. ...
95. laid*

96. (Poem)

UNIT III

97. praise*

98. Lorenzo*
    Hawkins'*
    Sara
99. frown*
    sharp*
    whiskers*
100. chose*
    comfortable*
    traveled*
101. spend*
    whittling*
102. ...
103. Dale*
104. drives*
105. chirped*
106. ...
107. buttons*
    pop*

108. question
109. either
    tears*
    cheeks*
110. bought*
    hidden*
    least*
111. Almighty*
    Thy*
    storms*
112. sinking*
113. ...

114. exclaimed*
115. discuss*
    spelling*
116. Barbara*
    Isidore*
    patron*
117. Spain*
    lad*
    instead*
118. plowed*
119. ...
120. miracle*
    creatures*

317

121. ...

---

122. Franz*
orchard*
123. described*
gowns*
mountains*
124. gathered*
wore*
125. sunrise*
clatter*
hoofs*
126. invitation*
pale*
127. ...
128. understand*
forward*
129. bit*
lips*
130. slept*
deeply*
tangled*
131. candles*
forgiveness*
132. paten*
133. realized*
134. gleaming*
chalice*
diamond*
135. ...
136. eternal*
glory*
Consecration*
137. ...

---

138. (Poem)

UNIT IV

139. ...

---

140. fortunes*
stupid*
able*
141. ant*
142. ponies*
marble*

143. ...
144. tablets*
enchantment*
thousand*
145. failed*
third*
whose*
146. key*
edge*
147. choose*
alike*
148. mouth*

---

149. granted*
150. ...
151. lies*
person*
exactly*
152. ...
153. onion
soup
beef*
154. satisfied*
155. cottage*
husband*

---

156. Marjory*
Marigold*
except*
157. beauty*
ugliness*
bone*
158. unpleasant*
guards
frosting*
159. snapped*
160. coach*
certainly*
south*
161. arrived*
162. interested*
163. ...
164. mirror*
165. ...
166. ...

---

167. nail*
beggar*
east*
168. ...
169. fellow*
stared*
170. meat*
171. stirring*
172. ...
173. oatmeal*

---

174. silver*
break
175. kingdom*
kick*
176. laughter*
177. ...
178. Rosebud*
medicine*
179. ...
180. led*
181. peeling*
kissed*
182. festival*
indeed*

---

183. CromDuv's*
Ireland*
Patrick*
184. ox*
quarters*
Deo Gratias
185. none
feed*
twelve*
186. message*
187. meant*
188. sword
189. anger*
horrible*
190. weighed*
scales*
191. calmly
192. ...

318

UNIT V
193. ...

---

194. won*
     tent*
195. calves*
     extra*
     hayfields*
196. health*
     eleven*
     unless*
197. sheep*
     peaches*
198. Leesburg*
     office*
     agent*
199. problems*
     sprayed*

---

200. leaned*
     squinted*
     branches*
201. perched*
     sort*
202. bushels*
203. blossoms*
     seventy-five*
204. touched
     June*
205. single*
     ripe*
206. dirty*
     thirty-seven*
     nap*
207. case*
     though*
     shrugged*
208. season*
     North*
209. ...
210. strength*
211. price*

---

212. (Poem)
213. Carter*
     chance*

214. ...
215. poultry
     bother*
216. awakened*
     shone*
     speckled*
217. ...
218. middle*
     electric*
     heater*
219. ...

---

220. empty*
     trunks*
     shape*
221. Andy's*
     crawling*
     beads*
222. agreed*
223. grinned*
224. sale*
     breathless*
225. pluck*
     number*
     settled*
226. lose
227. ...
228. slip*
229. woke*
     flown*
230. lamp*
231. quite*
232. coop*

---

233. crop*
     loaves*
234. understood*
     Savior*
     force*
235. ...
236. ...
237. Master*
238. everlasting*
239. ...
240. Flesh*

UNIT VI
241. ...

---

242. (Poem)
243. ...

---

244. Kristie*
     Elmer*
     Erik*
245. crooked*
     stuck*
246. hitched*
     brim*
247. ...
248. hired*
     borrow*
249. whinnied*
     tossed*
250. ...
251. nodded*

---

252. Banty*
253. ...
254. ...
255. ...
256. ...
257. jerk*
258. ...
259. fearfully*
     sore*
260. ...

---

261. kids*
     radio*
     announcer*
262. directions*
     playmate*
263. ...
264. ...
265. rang*
266. fat*
267. ...
268. ...

319

269. Pepper*
    ranch*
    limped*
270. doughnuts
271. trotting*
272. ...
273. pawed*
    gid-ap*
    gallop*
274. hang*
    whoa*
275. ...
276. ...
 	
UNIT VII
277. Carlos
    Mexico
    sombrero
 	
278. Beto's
279. Papa*
    turkeys*
    torn*
280. burro*
	281. Mama*
	282. ...
	283. coyotes
	284. ...
	285. ...
	286. ...
	
	287. cart*
	    Pedro
	288. wheels*
	289. ...
	290. shame*
	    Donno*
	291. ...
	292. ...
	293. ...
	294. ...
	295. oink*
	
	296. Juan
	    sandals*
	297. ...
	298. Pepe
	    spread*
		299. ...
		300. ...
		301. clay*
		302. ...
		303. ...
		304 scarf*
		
		305. kneeling*
		306. Virgin*
		    honor*
		    sight*
		307. ...
		308. ...
		309. ...
		310. ...
		311. blooming*
		312. wrapped*
		313. ...
		314. ...
		
		315. (Poem)

ABCDEFGHIJ 069876543
PRINTED IN THE UNITED STATES OF AMERICA